Breaking the Age Code

Young Skin for Life

Lesley Goodson

Shogo Ota (Graphic Designer)
Peter Economy (Editor)

This book is dedicated to my late father, Russel Goodson,
and most of all to my loving, incredible husband, Pierre.

Dog Ear Publishing
4011 Vincennes Road
Indianapolis, IN 46268
Visit our website at
www.DogEarPublishing.net

First trade edition February 2016.
ISBN 978-145754-313-5

CONTENTS

AUTHOR'S NOTE: The information in this book is not intended to be a substitute for medical and other professional advice; you are advised to contact your professional with regards to matters that require diagnosis or medical attention. This book includes medical experts' opinions which reflect independent judgement, formed without any payment or expectation.

The medical experts do not endorse or sponsor any products referred to in this book. The author believes that information in this book is accurate as of January, 2016. The publisher is not affiliated with the companies whose products or service are referred to in this book, does not endorse or sponsor any such products or services.

INTRODUCTIO

"You absolutely have to take this breakthrough anti-aging serum home today! It has more than six worldwide patents, and you won't believe how gorgeous your skin will look after using it!"

"How does it work? What's in it?" - you ask.

"This product has serious anti-aging properties," the salesperson responds. "Trust me, you'll love it!"

Sound familiar? Let's start with a typical trip to the cosmetics counter in any department store. There was a time when I was the salesperson on the other side of the counter—fresh from my two-day training seminar, and armed and excited about the miraculous potions that I would sell. I had access to all kinds of treatments from huge cosmetic companies, many with multiple worldwide patents. I was ready to come to the rescue of the people who would pay just about anything to stay young looking for as long as they possibly could.

Surely, with the millions of dollars their manufacturers committed to research and development, these products could buy us some degree of eternal youth. The only problem was the longer I worked as a cosmetics salesperson, the more I realized that the miracle of young skin was like a mirage—always just out of reach, an illusion. Over the years, I could see my own skin, as well as that of my clients, on a fast downward path to looking old. Products would come and go, but the hype and hope for younger-looking skin wouldn't.

IS THERE A BETTER WAY?

Along with the realization that the products I was selling—and personally using—weren't working, I experienced the dreaded moment in life that most every woman fears: the moment I was told by a friend at work that I had lost my youth!

SUDDENLY I'M OLD...HELP!!!

While I have always prided myself on staying fit and reasonably attractive, I was told, in a helpful way, of course, that I looked older than my mere 30 years. "What are you using around your eyes dear? Are you really just 31?" Upon closer inspection in the mirror, I noticed the serious beginnings of crow's feet around my eyes, and a general slackness in the skin of my face. I was devastated with the realization that I was aging—I felt like I was losing control because I felt too young to look so old. I had believed that my best days were ahead, and I ultimately came to the realization that I was right when I went on to a wonderful career in science, marketing, and pharmaceuticals.

And, along with this new career path, came a new personal path in my quest for younger-looking skin. Pharmaceutical training gave me the ability to break down the science, which led me to discover skincare strategies that have been a real miracle to me. And, yes, those crow's feet my co-worker pointed out are a thing of my past. I left them, and my co-workers, behind almost 30 years ago.

What followed my cosmetics sales job was a long career in pharmaceuticals. After lengthy training in virtually every disease state, as well as a graduate degree in marketing, I found myself working alongside many high-powered medical experts. We were educating, training, and breaking down complicated studies, and making the incomprehensible a possibility was my gift. I just loved the scientific aspect of my job, I loved diving into studies and sharing my discoveries with others. I was fortunate enough to have the opportunity to share many lengthy conversations with the nation's top dermatologists and aesthetic practitioners, and I was able to ask these experts the single question most women have wondered about for years: "What would you recommend as the best topical to keep skin youthful?" Nearly every expert I asked referred me to a variety of studies on specific, active compounds. Because they knew I was trained to dissect scientific studies, they would almost always reference them in their answers, sometimes even sending breakthrough studies to me as a small favor.

MY LIGHTBULB MOMENT

In my research, I realized that there was a lot of great data out there, and that there really were anti-aging substances available that really did work. Surely, I thought, the latest discoveries about what ages skin—along with breakthrough compounds to repair skin—must have made their way to the mainstream. So, after retiring from pharmaceuticals, I investigated the esthetician industry, thinking it might be a good second career. What I found was that they were still advertising the same old marketing myths I swallowed 30 years ago while working behind the counter. Nothing much had changed, and I didn't understand where the science was behind these myths.

Why was there so much scientific data available out there, but a huge disconnect when it came to being available to the public? I thought that everyone should have access to the latest discoveries and advances in the science of anti-aging.

Over time, I learned that there was a different path that people could take to generate younger skin— a path different from the mass-marketed skincare "secrets" that are splashed throughout almost every women's magazine and television talk show. This new path, which is the one that I present in this book for the first time anywhere, is based on scientific anti-aging breakthroughs that can truly transform skin, no matter what condition it's in.

In this book, I make all of these breakthroughs available to you, the reader, in an easy-to-read, fun, and straightforward fashion. I'll give you an inside look into your skin and how it works. You will be able to actually see the changes that take place in your skin as it ages. With this knowledge, based on the very latest scientific research and studies, you will be able to understand the big and little changes that lead to loss of radiance, discoloration, fragile withering, loss of firmness and, most important, wrinkling.

YOUR LIGHTBULB MOMENT

I have always thought that it was a shame the average person didn't have access to the newest scientific discoveries and breakthrough ingredients. After reading this book, you may never look at skincare the same way again, and I hope that you don't! If you truly care about aging skin, you first have to understand it—on all levels—before you can then tackle it head on, on a personal daily basis, instead of just during once-a-month visits to an esthetician.

I have personally experienced what a powerful effect science has had on my skin. I call it relying on the facts, not the fluff. I learned that the universal strategy of cleanse, tone, and moisturize will do absolutely nothing to stop or even slow down the aging process. I also embraced the power of supplements and nutrients. I've learned that there is power in knowledge, and it gives you a tremendous degree of control.

CHOOSE YOUR DESTINY

This book is designed to give you, the wonderful reader, control over your own skin's destiny. It's rewarding to take care of yourself, and it's even more rewarding to do so wisely, and with proper knowledge.

Chapter 1

THE MILLION DOLLAR QUESTION

IS SKIN AGING INEVITABLE?

ASK YOURSELF:

- **WOULD YOU LIKE TO BE A MEMBER OF THE "AGE-LESS" NOT THE "AGING GRACEFULLY" GROUP?**

- **WOULD YOU LIKE TO FEEL PROUD OF YOUR SKIN IN A ROOM FULL OF THIRTY-SOMETHINGS?**

- **DO YOU WANT TIME TO BE A DEAR FRIEND AND NOT YOUR ENEMY?**

- **DO YOU WANT TO LOOK FORWARD TO YOUR GOLDEN YEARS?**

01

IS SKIN AGING INEVITABLE?

WOULD YOU RATHER LOOK YOUR AGE OR LOOK AGELESS?

Aging skin impacts each and every one of us. Although some of us declare that we should all just accept it and aspire to age gracefully, deep down inside, if all of us were given the choice, we would opt for beautiful, youthful skin for life.

It's a harsh adjustment to watch ourselves metamorphose from our younger version to that of our elderly parents, or even our grandparents, no matter how much we love them. Smart people who don't want to helplessly stand by and watch as their skin slides into old age are the ones who turn to science-based articles and books confronting this tough issue. Science makes sense to them. They refuse to waste precious time reading books declaring flimsy promises.

And I'm sure you've heard them all.

Secrets to younger skin are promised through balancing the perfect pH, ancient acupuncture, a mind-spirit-body connection, or a special diet of rare organic fruits and vegetables—just feed your skin and starve away your wrinkles.

Savvy people know better because they understand that there's a vast expanse between science and silliness. Unquestionably, they realize that a healthy diet of fruits and vegetables, stress-free living, and

perhaps even an ancient facial acupuncture treatment thrown into the mix will most likely give them a more vibrant or even glowing appearance—any healthy lifestyle adjustment will.

But these savvy people are searching for results that go beyond aging gracefully. All the radiance in the world is not the same as a face with fresh, young, smooth, unwrinkled skin. No matter how healthy a lifestyle is created, in the end, there seems to be an inescapable skin-aging trajectory. Aging skin seems as unavoidable as death and taxes. Isn't aging skin inevitable?

FOCUS LIKE A LASER BEAM

Unfortunately, aside from a few science-based books—such as those written by Dr. Nicholas Perricone, which address significant aging solutions through cellular repair—most of the current skin-aging literature gloss over the critical ways our skin ages. They lose their focus. Perhaps because aging skin is a confluence of several confusing factors, the focus is switched to what is immediately understandable and recognizable. So, instead of focusing specifically on the biology of aging and scientifically proven treatments that reverse and guard skin from its effects, they instead focus on the treatment and handling of various skin types.

Sensitive, acne-prone, combination, and dryness issues—the *type* of skin fills many of the books designed to make you more beautiful. But skin typing is a different animal than skin aging. In the end, if we are too focused on controlling dry, oily, sensitive, or combination skin, we will miss the opportunity to provide our skin with the anti-aging strategy and treatments it needs to stay youthful, unlined, and beautiful. If your goal is to control the aging process, please don't confuse the two and lose focus. This book focuses like a laser beam on aging skin and how to control it.

Often, when the topic of aging is addressed, the answers you receive are nothing new—they seem to have the same ring to them.

• Avoid the sun's rays and tanning beds

• Use your moisturizer twice daily

• Eat more fruits and veggies

• Take time to de-stress

• Try yoga for a mind-body-spirit connection

But is there more you can do to control aging? Surely there is more to the story. Is there more you can learn?

In the real world, many of the answers to these questions do exist. The problem is the answers are typically found hidden within many of the National Institute of Health's (NIH) highly funded technical research studies. The good news is that the NIH has decoded much of the skin-aging puzzle. However, the average person would need a background in medical science and vast amounts of free time to make sense of the new discoveries by the NIH.

But, you might ask, isn't that the job of the cosmetic industry scientists?

Well, yes and no. While there has been some advancement in the cosmetic arena, they simply don't compare to the research testing being conducted in smaller, independent labs. There have been major strides made by scientists who are not constrained by agendas to develop products that satisfy the current marketing trends. You really need to know about these discoveries—there is so much more to this story and you'll be surprised by what you find out.

TIRED OF HEARING AGE OLD ADVICE ABOUT OLD AGE?

With modern science decoding more of the aging process, many of the older theories you may have read or heard about in the past are becoming less useful and even obsolete. These theories about the hows and whys of skin aging were grossly over-generalized, leaving you—the consumer—with few answers.

According to the older theories, the aging process comes down to two distinct and separate causal factors, or boxes, if you will.

INTRINSIC AGING

• Genetics

• Biological mechanisms

EXTRINSIC AGING

• UV rays

• Cigarette smoke

• Environmental toxins

It all basically boils down to this: we can avoid what harms us, and keep our fingers crossed that we were born with good genes—end of story. No more explanation needed or given. You might as well just turn the pages of your book and read about any topic other than aging.

Because doctors neatly place the reasons for our aging skin into two distinct boxes in an effort to answer the million-dollar question, we are missing what science can actually do to help our skin stay young. Much of what was thought to be uncontrollable is now within our control with treatments such as

• DNA repair enzymes

• Biomimetic hormone replacement

• Topical agents that can reverse precancerous lesions

And you are not warned about how the contents of the two boxes can spill out and overlap one another—causing a synergetic fast track to aging.

Menopausal women, for example, do not react the same way to sun exposure as they did in their youth, or even the same way as their husbands or boyfriends do who are the same age. They have not been warned of the synergetic effect that can lead to slack skin. Menopause is a uniquely vulnerable time in a woman's life when UV rays initiate a chemical cascade that targets the elastin network, with the result that what used to be a firm and taut neck and chin line become the complete opposite.

Please don't settle for oversimplification because there is so much more to this story. You will learn how so much of the aging process can be controlled and reversed by embracing the new body of knowledge, and this new body of knowledge can have powerful anti-aging results.

KNOWLEDGE OPENS DOORS, BUT YOU HAVE TO STEP THROUGH

Because we can't visualize the changes that are occurring within us, many of us struggle to understand what's below the surface of our skin. What's happening in the aging process to cause the changes we can see? This book is designed to open the door and allow you to visually understand the changes you face and how to reverse them. Yes, aging skin is a confluence of events, but confusing information simply makes more sense when explained visually.

An example of visual learning comes from Dr. Oz who, unlike any other physician today, uniquely presents visual concepts of many destructive diseases on his daytime television shows. Viewers love it because instead of a boring and confusing scientific dissertation, they can visually understand many of the medical issues they had previously left to the

medical community. This in turn helps them make better choices concerning their own healthcare, and the healthcare of their loved ones.

Scientific research doesn't need to be presented in a boring and difficult-to-understand dissertation fashion. As a visual learner myself, and a person who easily becomes bored by superfluous material, this book is intended to quickly get you, the reader, into a power mode where you can visualize your skin's changes as well as how topical solutions are working to correct those changes.

THE SECRET LIVES OF OUR SKIN CELLS

If you could look inside your skin with a powerful microscope, what changes would you see? In the Inside Skin chapter, you will first discover the structural changes happening below the surface of your skin that you see in the mirror each day. Why in your early thirties do you notice a slight yellowing in the color of your skin? Why do some parts of your skin—like your neck—look crepey, while other parts are smooth and appear fine? Why is there a loss of radiance, ashiness, or diminishing clarity from brown spots? Why are there pigment changes within your skin that never seem to go away, despite using all the skin lighteners that are available? Why are some age-related problems so stubborn and do we have to simply accept them?

And, finally, wrinkles—what we dread most of all, and the primary focus of this book—you will finally understand why you get them. No, wrinkles are not caused by dryness, and they do not result from using the wrong moisturizer. You will understand how your skin over time creates imperfect repairs that result in structural damage well below where your moisturizer travels. The result? Wrinkles.

You may never view your skin the same way again as you learn about parts of your skin you weren't even aware you had.

NEW STUDIES FOREVER CHANGE THE WAY YOU VIEW AGING

Midway through this book, you will find the scientifically established ways your skin creates the changes that begin the aging process. You will learn about:

• The toxic overload that overtakes your cells' defenses

• Destructive enzymes that start to go haywire in your thirties and beyond

• The hormonal reasons your skin becomes deprived of growth powers

• The real reasons UV rays damage your skin

• DNA altered repair consequences

After each reason behind the skin-aging process, you will read about significant age breakers to consider—new discoveries that can help you control the aging process. I've also added input from some of the country's most highly respected dermatologists and plastic surgeons.

FROM DAY 1 • YOU CAN:

- Open the locked doors and finally understand what's happening deep inside your skin as the years add up.

- Understand how your ethnic heritage contributes to your own unique aging process.

- Arm yourself with the facts that will prevent you from making the wrong treatment choices ever again.

- Discover secrets that have the power to reverse years of abuse and keep your skin looking young forever.

You will be presented with the best science-based and proven treatment strategies to date. You will learn how to smooth, strengthen, and stimulate your skin so that you can reverse much of the aged appearance you have accumulated, and even more important, lock your skin into a youth mode for life.

The combination of products you invest in is just as important as the manner in which you cleanse your skin twice each day. There are so many anti-aging products available today, but you need to learn which ones to choose. You will learn about the all-star skin stimulators, such as a powerful active that attaches to tiny skin cell receptors and creates youthful repair, and specific peptides and growth factors that trigger skin to go into a healthy repair mode. Because speed of learning is of the essence for your aging skin, you are given a birds eye view of what's proven to be most effective in the race against aging, and which products are the also-rans.

Finally, with so many skincare choices available, you need a survival kit to ensure you don't make mistakes by choosing products that won't improve your skin. The Skin Pearls will empower you by going into greater depth about all the topicals you may decide to purchase. From DNA repair enzymes to plant stem cells, you may be surprised by what you learn.

If various vitamins and plant essences have been researched, you can probably find them referenced within the Skin Pearls Glossary. If there's data about which strengths and formulations are more effective, you'll find that included there as well.

After reading this book, you will never view the process of aging skin the same way again. You'll find that you're able to control more of the aging process than you ever thought possible. The ultimate goal is to reverse the aged appearance of your skin, and then lock it into a youth mode for life. What does a youth mode entail? Being in youth mode means that the wrinkle machinery will cease, or at the very least, function at a snail's pace.

It's difficult for your skin to create wrinkles once you are in the youth mode. The fibroblasts that are responsible for creating the structural support of youthful skin will stay revved up, abundant, healthy, and active. Of course, a lot of these changes depend on you. If you adopt a few measures inside this book, you will see some improvement. I want you to maximize your skin's potential to reverse aging and stay young. This is why I give you general efficacy hierarchy scales to climb for maximizing results.

I want to give you the power to be proud of the skin you live in and for you to consider it one of your best assets. You don't have to settle for aging gracefully. Feeling good about your skin when you look in the mirror should be a normal, everyday occurrence. While aging prematurely myself, I, like many of you, have had those moments when young skin was a sweet memory. Losing control is no fun, and that's why I chose another path to follow—a path away from aging gracefully. I chose science for the healing powers it could bring. I took a leap of faith off the cosmetic train and into the world of scientific proof.

It paid off.

At 60 years old, my skin looks younger and has fewer wrinkles than it had at 30. What's more, with my treatment plan, I don't fear how my skin will look at 70—and you shouldn't either.

In life, our best years are always ahead of us. Having youthful skin just makes those years even better.

Discover what truly ages you and follow my Chapter 6, THE SYSTEM: SMOOTH • STRENGTHEN • STIM-ULATE for skin that looks wrinkle free, youthful, and vibrant for life. Guaranteed.

Chapter 2

INSIDE SKIN

WHAT'S YOUR SKIN STORY?

TURN THE PAGES TO GET A GRASP ON WHAT'S HAPPENING - AND CHANGING - INSIDE YOUR SKIN AS YOU AGE.

Did you know?

When it comes to aging, each layer of your skin has its own unique story to tell. While all the parts work together as a whole to protect you from the outside world, each layer declines differently as you age. Understanding the unique stories of your skin layers —the epidermis, DEJ, dermis, and hypodermis—will enable you to embrace new skincare advances and discard all the old notions, myths, and assumptions of the past.

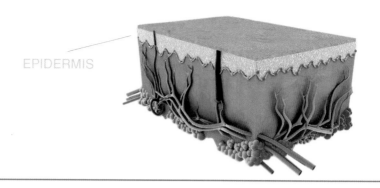

02

EPIDERMIS

The epidermis is the skin's outer structure that serves as the body's protector. It is the part that we see in the mirror each day, the horny layer, and is the end result of a 4-to-6-week process called keratinization. Keratinization is the process where cells are born in the lowest part of the epidermis, called the basal layer, and then undergo many changes as they migrate to the surface to be shed off. One of these changes causes the cells to become filled with a hardened protein called keratin. As the flattened, hardened keratin-filled cells are sloughed off, new cells are born just below in the basal layer. As we turn over in our beds, take showers, get dressed, or do anything that creates friction with the skin, we can shed up to nine pounds of cells every year.

One of the major functions of the epidermis is to prevent water loss from our skin. The epidermis produces lipids, which consist of ceramides, fatty acids, and other lipids acting as a cement between the bricks of keratin-filled cell layers. The combination of the two forms a waterproof barrier that acts to minimize trans-epidermal water loss (TEWL). The epidermis is sometimes referred to as the moisture barrier.

Another job of the epidermis is to protect us from outside invaders such as bacteria, chemicals, and other allergens or pathogens. One of nature's small miracles is giving this outer layer a slightly acidic pH (4.5 to 6.5). These slightly acidic layers of the moisture barrier are called the acid mantle. This acidity is due to a combination of secretions from the sweat- and oil-producing glands. Because the mantle is acidic, it inhibits the growth of fungi and bacteria within the skin. Another benefit of the acidity is that it helps maintain the hardness of the keratin-filled cells. When the skin's surface becomes alkaline,

the hardened cells become loose and soft, causing the skin to lose some of its protective properties. Using harsh soaps and detergents can make the skin more alkaline, making the skin more prone to infection and you may experience roughness and dehydration.

Like an army continuously protecting us from the outside world, your epidermis contains highly specific cells that are each designed with specific duties. Have you heard of melanocytes? These cells, found in the deepest layer of the epidermis, produce a substance called melanin. Melanin is the pigment that gives skin its color and helps protect you from the harmful effects of the sun. When you get a tan, it is the pigment that you see as darker skin or freckles.

"Think of your epidermis as your skin's gatekeeper. It keeps the bad stuff out and the good stuff in. Most products—including moisturizers—are unable to make it past the epidermis to where aging happens.

Scientists have come up with unique ways to induce good stuff like vitamin C, retinol, and growth factors to penetrate below this gatekeeper to the layers where true aging and wrinkles occur."

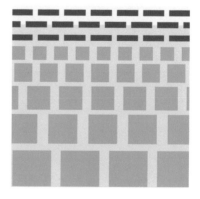

DERMAL EPIDERMAL JUNCTION

An important structure called the dermal epidermal junction (DEJ) is found at the junction between the dermis and epidermis. Often referred to as Nature's Velcro, the health and appearance of your skin will be determined by the condition of your DEJ. The DEJ interlocks the dermis to the epidermis by way of fingerlike projections called rete ridges. The waviness of the junction along the rete ridges increases the surface area available for the epidermis to receive nutrients from the dermis. Recall that the epidermis contains no blood vessels—it relies on the DEJ to receive the nutrients carried in the blood from the food and from the supplements we consume. If we are using a powerful anti-aging topical such as an antioxidant, retinoid, or peptide, the condition of the DEJ may determine the quantity of nutrients that reach the dermis. Maintaining a healthy relationship between the two layers of skin by way of the DEJ is key to maintaining young skin for life. Read on to learn about which skin conditions signal an unhealthy DEJ and the latest discoveries to help reverse it.

"Once believed to be an insignificant junction between your epidermis and dermis, the DEJ's wavy characteristic determines the levels of crepiness you'll experience on your neck and eye area as you age. Discover which actives target this critical layer."

DERMAL EPIDERMAL JUNCTION

EPIDERMIS

DERMIS

DERMIS

The dermis is located beneath the epidermis and is the thickest of the three layers of the skin. In fact, it makes up 90 percent of the skin's overall thickness. The main function of the dermis is to regulate temperature and to supply the epidermis with nutrients. Much of the body's water supply is stored within the dermis, which means that staying hydrated by drinking plenty of water throughout the day is important for your skin's appearance as well as overall health.

Unlike the epidermis, the dermis contains blood vessels. The blood vessels supply nutrients and oxygen to the skin, and the more of each of these supplied by the blood vessels, the healthier your skin will be. This is perhaps why the dermis can become thicker in individuals who both exercise and eat healthfully on a daily basis—their skin has received more oxygen and more nutrients. Exercise also increases human growth hormone (HGH), which is essential for youthful skin. Along with supplying skin with needed nutrients, the vessels also transport vitamin D produced in the skin to the rest of the body.

YOUR BUILT IN DETOX SYSTEM

Lymph vessels bathe the tissues of the skin with lymph, a milky substance that contains infection-fighting cells. As the lymph circulates to the lymph nodes, these cells work to destroy invading organisms or early infections much like an internal detox system. They also collect toxins that get eliminated when we sweat or urinate. Many estheticians incorporate lymphatic massage into a facial to encourage healthy movement of lymph through the system. Stress, inflammation, poor diet, and even water retention can make our lymphatic system sluggish.

The dermis also contains sebaceous or oil glands that are attached to hair follicles. The secreted oil helps keep skin smooth and supple. Your oils or lipids are a combination of fatty acids, ceramides, and cholesterol. These lipids form layers in and around skin cells creating a barrier that keeps natural moisture intact and prevents it from escaping. Many "barrier-repairing" moisturizers contain lipids that are similar to the intercellular lipids of the skin. The combinations of fatty acids, ceramides, and cholesterol in moisturizers may help to repair lipid bilayer membranes affected by soaps, solvents, and extreme dry or cold weather conditions by replacing key lipid components. The dermis also contains nerve endings that can transmit sensations of pain, itch, and pressure. If necessary, they can even trigger shivering if the skin senses that it needs to generate body heat.

Sweat glands not only keep us cool, but also rid the skin of topical pathogens and bacteria because they create what is referred to as the acid mantle. Sweat combined with oil produces a thin acidic film that keeps bacteria out of skin cells. If the mantle is temporarily removed by harsh soaps and sun damage, the skin becomes more susceptible to rashes and breakouts.

The most prevalent component of the dermis is the protein collagen. It forms a mesh-like framework—referred to as the "safety net"—that gives skin its strength, flexibility, and smoothness. Among the mesh of collagen fibers are moisture-binding molecules called glycosaminoglycans. These enable collagen fibers to retain water and provide moisture to the epidermis. Within the mesh is a smaller coiled protein called elastin. Much like a rubber band, elastin provides the skin with its ability to return to its original shape after stretching.

BIRTHPLACE OF A WRINKLE

As we age, the quantity and quality of the collagen and elastin network declines and this is the pivotal change in our skin that leads to the development of wrinkles. Luckily, the dermis—particularly the collagen safety net—is highly regenerative thanks to a type of cell called the fibroblast. Fibroblasts are your skin's manufacturing cells that produce the proteins, collagen, and elastin that provide structural support and elasticity to the skin and give it an unwrinkled appearance. In healthy skin, fibroblasts are numerous and can remanufacture more collagen fibers as well as divide and make more fibroblasts. Fibroblasts are also quite mobile and can move into a damaged area such as a scrape or scratch and reestablish the dermis where it is needed.

As the practice of skincare has become more scientific, researchers have discovered methods to make fibroblasts more productive. That's good news for all of us, as there are now effective treatments and techniques that really do work to dial back the hands of time when it comes to our skin.

"Home of your skin's SAFETY NET—the collagen, elastin network or "NET" that keeps your skin young, firm, and wrinkle free. You'll discover the latest scientific research about what things keep it youthful and productive—and what things don't."

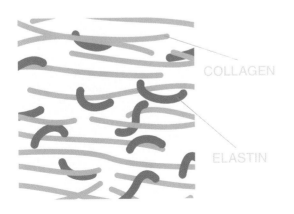

COLLAGEN

ELASTIN

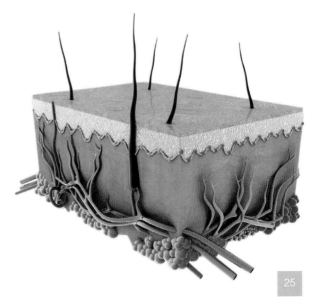

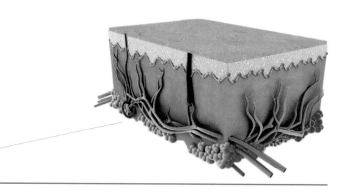

HYPODERMIS

The deepest layer of skin, which is called the hypodermis—the fat layer—serves to cushion the body and regulate our body temperature. While it is made mostly of fat tissue and fibrous bands that anchor skin to the deep fascia, the hypodermis serves to nourish the dermis through connecting blood and lymphatic vessels, and hair follicles. It is full of nerves, important glands, and fine sheets of muscle.

There is a certain type of aging attributed to a natural loss of fat called hypodermis aging, and it happens to most of us. This type of aging is marked by the loss of fat tissue that ultimately affects the shape of our faces and hands. Cheeks and eye sockets may become hollow, and the skin on the neck, hands, and arms may lose its firmness. With this progression, our faces seem to lose the soft contours of our youth. Researchers have found a way to use soft fillers to rejuvenate almost any area on the body that has become hollowed from aging. Fat transfers are becoming increasingly popular as an alternative to more-invasive surgery to return that soft bloom of youth to facial contours.

A NATURAL SOLUTION TO REGAIN VOLUME AND YOUTHFUL CONTOURS

But are there other alternatives?

Another popular solution that you may have encountered in your search for an answer is facial exercise. If you look up facial exercise on the Internet, everyone seems to have an opinion as to the possible benefits of the practice. While some experts such as Dr. Oz and Dr. Perricone endorse facial exercising, not all do. Many dermatologists and plastic surgeons are against facial exercising because they believe that the repetitious squinting and pulling of the skin encourages wrinkling. Perhaps in some methodologies and books these facts are true, but there are other highly effective methods that don't involve either of the above.

I am particularly happy to have the opportunity to endorse a form of facial exercise developed by Carole Maggio. I had first seen her on YouTube and decided to give a few of her exercises a try by starting with two of her jaw-firming exercises. As women age, due to muscle slackness and loss of the fat layer, our jawline becomes more of a square shape instead of V-shape. After skeptically committing to just the jaw exercises, I experienced amazing results in a very short period of time. As I included more exercises from Carole's regimen, I watched my face achieve the soft contours I so very much missed from my youth, and the tissue felt plumper and firmer. Since then, I have incorporated more of her exercises into my daily regimen. Facial exercises will never replace great skin, but they work amazingly well alongside other preventative and restorative measures. You can achieve great skin, but if the tone underneath your skin is slack, you may feel that you are only able to control half of the anti-aging battle. Facial exercise can pick up the slack, and while it is still a bit embarrassing to talk about because it is so new to society, it truly can be transforming to your face. I highly recommend Carole Maggio's book, *Ultimate Facercise*, to anyone looking into facial exercise.

"Does a woman need to eventually decide between her face or her body? Read on about the ways fat loss ages our faces. But don't despair—better, and more effective remedies are emerging. Forget the face lifts — facial exercises, fat transfers and better fillers can transform sagginess into youthful contours."

Chapter ☐3

A CLOSER LOOK:
WHAT'S YOUR CONCERN?

Whatever your concern we now live in an age where almost any concern is not only preventable but treatable. Turn the pages for a closer look...

LOSS OF RADIANCE

DISCOLORATION

LOSS OF FIRMNESS

WRINKLES

BROWN SPOTS

SPIDER VEINS

DARK CIRCLES

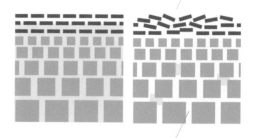

LOSS OF RADIANCE

IT'S ALL ABOUT LIGHT

Think of light reflecting off a still lake at the break of dawn. How well light bounces off the surface of your skin will determine your degree of radiance. Along with good nutrition and exercise, creating a luminous appearance is all about adding a good moisturizer, and ensuring you're getting the right amount of exfoliation.

Women tend to notice a loss of radiance earlier in life than men do. It becomes apparent to women as they realize that their makeup doesn't look as fresh and their foundation begins to fade within a couple hours. Their makeup is being absorbed into the accumulated dead skin cells. Skin looks dull and creates other havoc when dead skin cells build up on its surface. The buildup gives a very tired and unhealthy appearance to skin. When skin is in top form, fair skin should have a rosy gleam to it and darker complexions should have a luminosity. This is a sign that skin is getting adequate blood flow with a healthy rapid turnover of surface cells. But as we age, a surface buildup of dead cells inhibits the natural glow we see from a healthy circulation. What happens?

Up to the age of 14, our skin exfoliates naturally every 14 days. The quick rate of renewal leaves children with a healthy-looking glowing complexion. However, with the passage of time, the rate of natural exfoliation slows down. By the age of 25, the rate of exfoliation doubles to 28 days, and after that it can even increase to a whopping 75 days. The resulting buildup of dead cells leaves skin looking like flat paint rather than a glowing surface. When dead skin cells build up on the surface of skin, they scatter light, making skin appear lifeless and dull.

No matter what our age, deep in the epidermis, in the basal layer, new cells are being generated every day. As a cell is born, soon there is another cell born underneath it, and one more after that and another and another. During their forced journey to skin surface, they undergo a lot of changes. One of those changes is to become filled with a hardened substance called keratin. Eventually these keratin filled, toughened cells called corneocytes become embedded in a glue like matrix. This matrix sticks the cells together similar to bricks and mortar. As a result your skin cells become an effective, tough barrier between you and the environment.

YOUR SKIN'S BUILT-IN SMOOTHING SYSTEM

As new cells are continually being born the outermost cells need to be sloughed off. Otherwise our skin would be inches thick. Researchers have discovered that our skin generates specific enzymes that helps the surface cells separate from each other in a process called *desquamation*. The catch is that these enzymes need hydration to thrive and be effective. As our oil production slows with

age, especially during menopause, our skin starts to lack the enzymes that help the desquamation process. With more and more buildup of dead cells, radiant skin becomes only a memory.

So forget the classic cleanse, tone, moisturize you learned in your 20s. If you could make one major change in your skincare regimen, it would be to replace cleanse with exfoliation. Exfoliation is key to keeping your skin looking energized in your 30s and beyond. You've probably read about or heard that exfoliating once or twice weekly is key to keeping your skin vibrant. However, experts in the field of anti aging are advising daily exfoliation. Why? Because the benefits of daily exfoliation are almost too numerous to list. The process not only helps maintains radiance, it allows products to penetrate, and increases the dermal matrix of collagen and elastin giving it the spring it had in its youth. It also increases the number and size of collagen-producing cells called fibroblasts. The more fibroblasts, the younger your skin will appear. I like to replace the term skin cleansing with skin "smoothing". A daily exfoliation will deliver immediate smoothing effects as well as firming, anti-wrinkle smoothing in weeks and years to come.

A CLOSER LOOK AT THE BENEFITS OF DAILY EXFOLIATION

Skeptical? Lets have a closer look at a group of people who exfoliate their skin daily. The group I am referring to is men who shave. Without even realizing it, men exfoliate their skin every day through the simple act of shaving. The scraping of the blade against the skin removes the dead, hardened layers. Observe the face of a middle aged man who shaves regularly and who most likely doesn't moisturize. You'll notice there's a disparity in the quality of the skin on the forehead and around the eyes compared to that around the lips and jaw line. On the forehead and eye area, there are mostly wrinkles and other telltale signs of aging when compared to the rest of the face.

The difference you see is because daily exfoliation not only increases cellular turnover in the epidermis, it also stimulates the lower layer, the dermis to go into repair mode and generate more collagen and elastin. This results in smooth, youthful-looking skin. Did you notice I remarked that men rarely moisturize their facial skin? While moisturizing is important to skin health in general, if you want your skin to be unwrinkled, vibrant, and smooth, exfoliation should be your number-one priority. No matter how often you moisturize, a moist skin will not keep wrinkles at bay. Wrinkles originate deep within the dermis where moisturizers don't reach. We are truly lucky that such a simple task as exfoliation can reap such major anti-aging benefits.

BRIGHTEN UP

As more experts are embracing exfoliation as, without a doubt, the most important step in any good skincare regimen, there has been controversy as to the most effective way to remove the superficial layer of dead skin cells that stand between you and radiant skin. Basically, there are two methods available – manual exfoliation and chemical exfoliation. Manual exfoliation includes buff puffs, electric brushes, cleansing grains and beads. They remove dead cells by scraping away at the surface. Chemical exfoliants (like alpha hydroxy acid) remove dead skin cells by "dissolving" the glue that binds them together. Other chemical exfoliants include B-hydroxy acids, salicylic acid and fruit enzymes. Refer to your Skin Pearls Glossary to read about what to look for, the plusses and the minuses.

DID YOU KNOW?

That African-American skin has a more compact stratum corneum than many other ethnicities? A compact stratum corneum creates superior cohesion, which helps generate a smoother skin surface. This is one of the reasons behind the luminous skin quality of stars such as Halle Berry, Queen Latifah, Lupita Nyong'o, and Viola Davis.

SKIN SAVVY

• Getting rid of dead cell buildup is a surefire way to ensure light is evenly reflected off your skin. Exfoliation will make your skin look luminous and brilliant!

• Did you know? Our skin has its own built-in system to exfoliate itself and ensure skin looks radiant. This built-in system consists of enzymes that break apart the dead cell buildup. When everything works, we glow!

• The catch is that our enzymes need moisture to thrive. That's why dry skin encourages dullness. Skin that lacks moisture makes those precious enzymes that encourage radiance disappear—a double whammy!

• Who lacks those precious enzymes most? Sad but true, menopausal women lack the enzymes required for natural exfoliation to take place. A good moisturizer is a must!

• Getting rid of dead cell buildup—along with using a good moisturizer—is also a must for anyone who wants to ditch dullness. You'll learn more about this vital step in Chapter 6, THE SYSTEM: SMOOTH • STRENGTHEN • STIMULATE.

RECOMMENDATIONS

THE NEW ERA

A new era of skin smoothing is here! Experts are continually bumping up their recommended levels of exfoliation, taking us beyond what we may have encountered in the past. That's good news for all of us who want to maintain radiance and reap the myriad anti-aging benefits it can bring. Sonic brushes, buff puffs, AHA pads, glycolic and enzyme cleansers, and high-tech facial cloths are emerging rapidly. As you'll read later, I recommend and am a big fan of physical exfoliation. The reason I prefer it is because I have seen better and more reliable results, including:

- Superior long-term, anti-wrinkle effects

- Less tricky to use than AHAs, with more consistent results

- Allows you to easily adjust the amount of exfoliation

USE MORE OF THIS

Bobbi Brown© Buffing Grains for the Face

$43.00 - *BobbiBrownCosmetics.com*

A bottle of luxurious grains that can be mixed and customized with your favorite cleanser.

Sephora® Collection, Metamorphosis Exfoliating Powder

$20.00 - *Sephora.com*

A gentle, micro-cellulose powder scrub that can be mixed with your daily cleanser.

Josie Maran - Gentle Exfoliating Powder

$35.00 - *JosieMaranCosmetics.com*

Gentle enough even for the most sensitive skin. Can even be used with your Clarisonic.

Clarisonic - Sonic Cleansing Brush

starts at $99.00 - *Clarisonic.com*

The latest trend—and a good one.

BeautyProof® - YoungME VitaC Smoothing Grains

$36.00 - *BeautyProof.com*

The ultimate step in halting wrinkles and amazingly diminishing the ones you already have. Designed to be used on an as-needed basis in conjunction with your cleanser. Expect remarkable skin-smoothing effects in as little as one week.

Brilliant buys on a budget...
Salux Body Cloth

$5.98 - *SaluxCloth.com*

A 60% nylon 40% polyester Japanese bathing exfoliating cloth that was named a Japan National Invention Award winner. Long lasting, extremely effective, and more sanitary than a washcloth.

Exfolia Disposable Microexfoliation Facial Cloths

$12.00 20/pack - *SkinMedix.com.*

Nano-scale fibers remove dead skin cells without intrusion or damage to the lower layers of the epidermis. A marvel of German technology—five years in development, and a favorite of mine!

Body Benefits - Exfoliating Facial Sponge

$2.00 - *Ulta.com*

Probably one of the best-priced beauty bargains around. I've never been without one.

USE LESS OF THIS

Square-edged exfoliants such as sugars and salts. Save these for rougher areas of your body, or better yet, just invest in a Salux body cloth.

Jagged-edged exfoliants such as fruit seeds and nut shells are not good for skin of any type. That's because these can cause irritation, and even worse, a sheering of your epidermal protective barrier.

Exfoliating sponges that aren't effective. Natural sponges such as konjac (actually made from the roots of an Asian vegetable) are now the rage, but don't be fooled and buy into the marketing claim that they enhance radiance in any way. They may be lovely to use, are often infused with aloe or green tea, but they are too smooth to have a beneficial effect. Sad for something so lovely and natural.

CREPINESS

Most people know crepey skin when they see it. The area from the chin to the bust is particularly prone to its appearance. It tends to suddenly show up when we least expect it. One moment we look fine in our summer camisole, the next we seem to be wearing a much older persons skin. Some say it is the face that gives away a person's age and troubles us the most but it actually is the neck that make us most unhappy when we look in the mirror. Once thought to be untreatable, science has made huge strides in understanding why we get this particular type of wrinkling, and more important, how to reverse it.

In fact, as the field of cosmecueticals grows, researchers are zeroing in on specific strategies for alleviating many specific types of wrinkles such as crepiness. Future skincare will no longer be a cookie-cutter approach as treatments become more focused and effective.

A CLOSER LOOK

But lets have a closer look at crepiness. What makes this type of wrinkling unique? Crepey skin is different from permanent wrinkles in that the skin appears crinkled, fragile, and paper thin. When you pull the skin at each side, the tiny wrinkles tend to flatten out. This type of wrinkling is highly associated with old age. In the past, treatment consisted of rich emollients to protect the fragile area with perhaps the addition of a few nutrients and caffeine to kick start the fragile skin. Sadly, these concoctions did little to nothing to fix the problem. In reality, this is a unique type of skin aging that requires highly specific, laser beam treatment to be effective.

Where does crepey skin come from? New findings attribute its onset due to the breakdown of the area where the dermis and epidermis meet. Have you noticed that as you get older, you're more prone to get cuts and scratches and your skin just shears more easily than it did when you were younger? Scientists attribute this to a flattening of the dermal epidermal junction. The dermal epidermal junction or DEJ is nature's unique Velcro that connects and anchors your lower dermis to the upper epidermis. Notice its wavy appearance in the young skin illustration. This waviness increases the surface area so that the epidermis or top layer has more room to receive nutrients from the dermal or lower area where the blood supply and nutrients reside. The structural change or flattening effect reduces the surface area for nutritional exchange and metabolic byproducts evacuation. As a consequence, epidermal cell turnover slows down and free radicals accumulate. Restoring the cell-matrix interactions at the DEJ can greatly improve and strengthen frail, withered skin.

What causes its breakdown leading to the fragile withered appearance we all dread? Let's look at new research findings. Although researchers admit there is much more to be learned, they have discovered that in order for a youthful DEJ to be intact, the proteins that support it need to be strong and healthy. These supportive proteins, called laminins and fabrils, are specific subtypes of collagen. In a healthy DEJ they are responsible for maintaining its unique wavy architecture that give us healthy, smooth, strong, skin. Although a flattened DEJ is associated as an inevitable consequence of intrinsic aging, researchers were amazed at how rapidly solar radiation breaks down these proteins (lamins and fabrils) that play a huge role in your skin's appearance. UV radiation activates protein-digesting enzymes termed collagenase and metalloproteinases that oh so rapidly eat away at these delicate and hugely important network of supportive proteins.

BETTER TREATMENTS

The exciting news is that the new discoveries have brought about treatments designed to target and repair the damage. Unique peptides as well as growth factors have been developed that are highly specific to encouraging the growth and repair of these particular proteins. Reconstruction of the DEJ is greatly enhanced by these new treatments. This makes much of the once permanent damage reversible. Quantifiable measurements prove that they are effective! What follows is a list of products with peptides formulated to repair your DEJ

HEALTHY DEJ

UNHEALTHY
FLATTENED DEJ

A flattened DEJ means that fewer nutrients are passed between the dermis and the epidermis.

"Peptides that target the DEJ are highly effective and proven to help turn a crepey neck into a smooth one. Ensure your neck treatment includes one of these newer compounds that don't rely on older formulations."

RECOMMENDATIONS

WHY YOU SHOULD INVEST

Many of you may have read or heard that you are wasting your money if you purchase neck treatments and creams, because the skin on your neck is the same as the skin on your face and on the rest of your body. While it is true that the basic structure of your skin is exactly the same, the skin on your neck is much thinner and much more reliant on a tight cohesion between your upper and lower layer—the DEJ—in order to maintain a smooth appearance. In other words, a flattening of the DEJ in thin skin—such as the skin on your neck—is easier to detect. If the cohesion goes, so does the smoothness of your skin. What's more, your neck skin does not have the skeletal and muscular support that your face does.

A WORD OF ADVICE

These recommended formulations may appear expensive, but it's important to remember that the most expensive skincare products are the ones that don't work. The formulations listed below are worth the investment! Nothing ages a woman like a crepey neck. It's a calling card that you're a member of the "aging gracefully" and not the "ageless" club—and you declined membership in the former, remember?

SKIN SAVVY

One of the first signs of aging is crepiness. This happens when the cohesion between the two outermost layers of our skin breaks down. As the cohesion weakens, crepiness first appears in the neck and eye area where skin is the thinnest, and unsupported. Be smart and invest in products designed to repair this unique type of aging. Most store-bought moisturizers do little to address this issue and are a waste of your hard-earned money. Save your pocketbook and your neck!

Rethink soy. A simple daily supplement of 40mg/d isoflavones really delivers! Studies show significant repair from this simple regimen. Just another reason Asian women age so beautifully!

DHC Neck Treatment Essence Peptides

$42.00 - *DHCCare.com*

Includes one of the most powerful peptides available, Matrixyl 3000. This essence tones and boosts elasticity around the neckline and décolleté.

Elemis Pro - Collagen Lifting Treatment for Neck

$117.00 - *Elemis.com*

Packs a powerful punch of botanical extracts, oils, and peptides. Independent studies show a 33 percent decrease in crepey-like skin. Another winner.

NeoStrata® Skin Active Triple Firming Neck Cream

$79.00

Uses three advanced ingredients to smooth and firm the neck area. It helps build volume as well as stimulates repair of the collagen matrix.

Dr. Brandt Skincare Do Not Age with Dr. Brandt Firming Neck Cream

$65.00 - *DrBrandtSkincare.com*

A blend of advanced peptides and other actives powered by Dr. Brandt's advanced delivery system. Consumers report a firmer, smoother, more-lifted appearance.

BeautyProof® - Micro Lift Neck Repair

$68.00 - *BeautyProof.com*

An extraordinary cream that delivers a dramatic increase in neck density. As volume is restored, skin is revitalized, tightened, and lifted. Dramatic reduction in crepiness can be seen in 28 days.

WRINKLES

"We are all aware that the sun gives us premature wrinkles, but were you also aware that the sun gives us wrinkles that are much more predominant? Here's the story..."

It is an admitted truth that wrinkles are the number-one manifestation of aging that people hate most. Even young people hate wrinkles because it gives them the sense that they are running out of time. There is a common belief that no matter how clean and healthy your lifestyle, like death and taxes, sooner or later your skin will lose its youthful tone. Because of this, anti-wrinkle treatments can be found in almost everyone's medicine cabinet.

GENETICS MATTER

The manifestations of wrinkling and skin aging depend largely on genetic factors. Fair-skinned Caucasians have a much higher propensity toward wrinkle development than other ethnicities. African Americans, Asians and other darker skinned ethnicities are more prone to develop freckles, sunspots, and other pigmentation problems.

Even with the discrepancies, you are still told that wrinkles are inevitable and your best option is to delay their occurrence. However, with recent scientific breakthroughs, wrinkled skin can not only be almost totally prevented, it can also be greatly reversed.

A MAJOR BREAKTHROUGH

One of the major breakthroughs was a landmark study conducted in France and published in the *British Journal of Dermatology.* The purpose of the study was to go deeper into the knowledge of skin's structural changes underlying the development of wrinkles in both sun-exposed and sun-protected areas. If researchers discovered what goes wrong in skin, they could develop treatments to halt and even reverse the problem! I hope that after you read this, it may change the way you think about the current wrinkle treatments. There are serious changes taking place. Changes that can be controlled if

you choose the right treatments and not the wrong ones. This book is dedicated to helping you make the right decisions.

SEEING IS BELIEVING

Researchers took a deep look at roughly 157 biopsies of wrinkles in ages 57 to 98. They pulled out all the stops using a multitude of discovery techniques including electron microscopy, image analysis, and techniques involving histological chemistry to name a few. Using a multitude of methods, they examined wrinkles in many parts of the body. The findings show intense structural changes deep below the skin's surface. You will learn later why these changes occur and how to thwart and even reverse the damage.

ANATOMY OF A WRINKLE 101

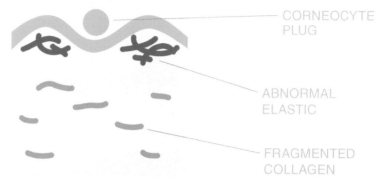

CORNEOCYTE
PLUG

ABNORMAL
ELASTIC

FRAGMENTED
COLLAGEN

HEALTHY SKIN

Skin has a healthy network of collagen and elastic fibers. Similar to a "Safety Net," the collagen network provides supportive, smooth, plump skin.

UV WRINKLE

The sun generates an abundance of abnormal elastic tissue that "flanks" the wrinkle, making it appear deeper and coarser.

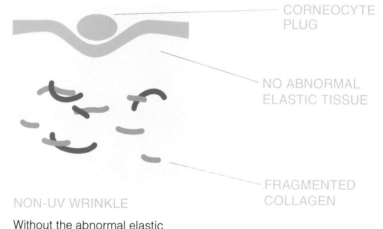

CORNEOCYTE
PLUG

NO ABNORMAL
ELASTIC TISSUE

FRAGMENTED
COLLAGEN

HEALTHY SKIN

Skin has a healthy network of collagen and elastic fibers. Similar to a "Safety Net", the collagen network provides supportive, smooth, plump skin.

NON-UV WRINKLE

Without the abnormal elastic tissue, the wrinkles are less severe. Hormonal changes, a sugary diet and free-radical damage all lead to a loss of the supportive "Safety Net."

1. CORNEOCYTE PLUG

Researchers were surprised to find that almost all wrinkles regardless of sun damage had a thickened accumulation of corneocytes, or dead skin cells. You may recall that these are the keratin-filled, hardened cells on the very top layer of your skin whose function is to provide an effective barrier between you and the environment. Your skin naturally sheds these dead skin cells, but as you age, the process slows down. Step 1 in THE SYSTEM: SMOOTH • STRENGTHEN • STIMULATE is exfoliation, or as I call it, smoothing. Removing dead skin cells through daily skin smoothing is like erasing a small portion of the wrinkle, and it may explain why men who shave with razor blades have such smooth and youthful skin.

2. THINNING OF THE EPIDERMIS

Although the thickness of skin is variable depending on the body localization, the thickness of the epithelium was diminished directly underneath a wrinkle. Experts ask if wrinkles could be caused by the thinning epithelial tissue. This was not the case. They believe that the epithelial tissue is compressed after the wrinkle is created as the number of cell layers remains the same as in smooth skin.

"Just as an illness can't be cured or prevented until it is fully understood, the exact same thing is true for wrinkles. The discovery of the deep structural changes responsible for wrinkles is one of the most important cosmetic research discoveries of the 21st century. Better understanding has led to better, more effective treatments."

3. FLATTENING OF THE DERMAL EPIDERMAL JUNCTION

You may recall the vital role the DEJ plays for maintaining youthful, beautiful skin. In young skin, it has a wavy pattern, allowing more surface area for nutrients to transfer and wastes to evacuate. When the DEJ flattens, there is less cohesion between the layers. Skin is less resilient and compact. In fact, a flattening of the DEJ is the first major change that happens deep inside skin that leads to crepiness in the neck and around our eyes. The linear development is due to the breakdown of the proteins called anchoring fibrils that support it.

4. ATROPHY OF COLLAGEN MATRIX

Even if skin has had a general loss of collagen, the breakdown of the collagen network is more marked under a wrinkle than in the surrounding area. As you'll soon learn in Chapter 5 Why we Age collagen loss and damage is due to a variety of factors. A sugary diet, hormonal changes, free radicals, and UV activated enzymes, to name a few.

5. INCREASE IN ABNORMAL ELASTIC TISSUE

Researchers were startled to find that wrinkles caused by UV rays actually had a surprising increase and not decrease of elastic tissue, whereas UV-protected skin had fewer elastic fibers occurring with age. In sun-damaged skin, the abnormal elastic tissue formed in bundles and flanked on the sides of wrinkles (not underneath) boosted the magnitude and depth of each wrinkle. You may have heard of actinic elastosis. This is an extreme condition of UV damage we all want to avoid. When you notice the coarseness' and yellowed appearance of sun worshippers skin, what you are seeing is the result of an extreme accumulation of the nonfunctional elastic tissue flanking every wrinkle. Sun goddesses beware!

As we dive into the causes of the changes you see above that lead to wrinkles, you'll read about treatments that truly work, and you'll probably learn why what you are currently using just isn't all that effective. For example, you probably have been told that the retinol you purchase from the drug store is the same as prescription retinoid (Retin A) but without all the irritating side effects. That's just not the case. The differences are so great that some dermatologists have spoken out that the retinol you find in the drugstore or cosmetic counter is only about one twentieth the efficacy as Retin A. There are better options and that's what this book is about. Some novel products are beginning to emerge. For example a better retinol called retinaldahyde is showing rejuvenating skin benefits similar to the robust benefits of the prescription Retin A and a few product lines are incorporating it into their skincare lines. You'll also learn that it takes a combined approach using proper exfoliation as well as dermal stimulators to bring your skin back to a significantly youthful appearance. Some prevent or shield cells from damage. Some interact with the cellular DNA. Some trigger cells to go into youth mode and start replacing damaged collagen with healthy collagen.

Treating wrinkles is a process you will learn about in my proven THE SYSTEM: SMOOTH • STRENGTHEN • STIMULATE. Therefore, I do not list product recommendations at this time. Along with a unique treatment strategy, you'll learn how various anti-aging products - growth factors, peptides, alpha hydroxy acids — to name a few, work in the war on wrinkles and how to incorporate them in your daily skincare. You'll also learn what strengths are effective and what ones aren't. Beautiful, smooth skin is within everyone's reach.

RECOMMENDATIONS

Now you've discovered why it's so important to protect and shield your skin from UV rays. You'll discover later on about how even just 15 minutes of sun exposure can trigger aging consequences that result in hours and even days of aging events inside your skin. In comparison to the lines and creases caused by free-radical exposure, a sugary diet, hormonal changes—and even inflammation—being kissed by the sun too many times will leave behind wrinkles that are…

• **Deeper.** Because discarded and abnormal elastic material builds up on its flanks.

• **Wider.** Because as the elastic material continues to accumulate, wrinkles widen.

• **More permanent.** Because lines created by other causes of aging are easier to repair.

• **Leathery texture.** Because of the buildup of discarded elastin, your skin becomes thicker.

Remember that when it comes to wrinkles, deeper, wider, and leathery is a bullet train ticket to the aging not-so-gracefully club. A day without protection from the sun's rays can yield hazardous—and lifelong—consequences.

Don't let this be you.

A femme française once said,

"Beauty is not a gift, it is a habit."

THE 3 BEAUTY ESSENTIALS THAT BELONG IN EVERYONE'S HANDBAG.

1. A self-adjusting powdered mineral sunscreen for facial touchups.

All the doctors and experts agree that few of us use adequate levels of SPF to fully protect our skin. This one, brilliant product gives you that extra UV protection your skin deserves. Brilliant because it does not upset your makeup, it's easy to use, and it makes your skin look fresher throughout the day. Make a habit of touching up every time you reapply your lip gloss. Just tap the wand, brush, and go. You don't even need to wait 30 minutes for protection.

Colorscience® Sunforgettable® Sunscreen SPF 30
$52.00 (refill $39.00) - *Colorscience.com*

Available in many shades and lasts forever. Just remember to tap before you use it.

Peter Thomas Roth Oily-Problem Skin Instant Mineral SPF-30
$30.00 - *PeterThomasRoth.com*

Oil-free translucent brush-on powder for immediate anytime UVA/UVB protection. Willow bark extract and vitamins A,C and E added.

2. A hand cream with an SPF of at least 15.

Not as easy to find as you would think. Use a hand cream every time you wash during the day. If you pick one that feels and smells luxurious—like Deborah Lippmann's "Rich Girl" hand cream—you'll look forward to its spa-like qualities.

Deborah Lippmann "Rich Girl"
Hand Cream SPF 25
$28.00 - *Sephora.com*

Formulated with shea butter, avocado, and jojoba oil. Contains botanical brighteners to help maintain an even skin tone.

L'Occitane® Brightening Hand Care SPF 20
$30.00 - *LOccitane.com*

A triple-action formula containing many essential oils from the Provence area of Southern France. Just like the region it's from, it smells heavenly.

Neutrogena® Age Shield Hand Cream SPF 30
$6.00 - *Drugstores*

Very well loved for its luxurious texture and rejuvenating results. It contains anti-agers as well as broad-spectrum protection, which is what you're after.

3. Sunglasses

What has become a status symbol can also help save the delicate skin around our eye area. If you feel and look glamorous, not to mention experiencing the "hip" factor, you're more apt to use them.

If left unprotected, the delicate eye area will age rapidly. The sun, along with squinting, is a sure way to get what we would rather do without—crow's feet.

Tip: You can discover a treasure chest of high-end designer sunglasses on the listed sites. Although you can't try on the glasses before you purchase them, they are returnable, are a click away, and won't break the bank.

• Gilt.com

• MyHabit.com

Keeping your skin wrinkle free—and regressing the ones you've accumulated over the years—is a process I reveal in the THE SYSTEM: SMOOTH • STRENGTHEN • STIMULATE chapter. Don't worry, you'll discover which products and methods truly have the power to both repair and regress wrinkles created from all the things that life throws our way! Read on to learn more about products that truly make a difference.

WHAT TO LOOK FOR...

Products containing the right kind of peptides.

What do I mean by the right peptides? The answer is simple. There are many peptides available, but the ones that reverse wrinkles and significantly bump up collagen production are known as "signal" peptides. These wonders trick your skin into thinking it needs to go into an aggressive repair mode, and they outperform vitamin C—not for their protective effect, but also for their stimulating effect on your safety net of collagen and elastin. Refer to your Skin Pearls Glossary for more information.

Olay Regenerist Micro Sculpting Serum,
Local Pharmacy

$25.99 - *Local pharmacy*

A relatively inexpensive anti-wrinkle serum, using many of the same ingredients found in higher-end products. Recommended by many dermatologists because you get the science without the high price tag.

Strivectin® Potent Wrinkle Reducing Treatment

$99.00 - *Strivectin.com*

A serum charged with collagen- and elastin-stimulating peptides, as well as detoxifying plant cells. The company's most technologically advanced product to date.

Exuviance® Collagen Triple Boost Serum

$72.00 - *Neostrata.com*

A plumping serum containing a potent collagen stimulator, called Matrixyl . Combined with amino acids and neo glucosamine, it also blocks the enzymes that break down your dermal matrix.

BeautyProof ® CELLXCELL Lifting
+ Firming Serum

$89.00 - *BeautyProof.com*

A pioneering formula of newly discovered "signal" peptides that trigger skin to dramatically increase density and elasticity. Praised for its effectiveness to firm and tone all facial contours including jawline. An unprecedented formula containing 99% peptides.

A MORE EFFECTIVE RETINOL

Don't all retinols work the same? Well, they do and they don't. The problem is in the journey. And for almost all the store bought retinols, it's a long one—very long. Not only the length of the journey, but the likelihood your skin has the capability to remanufacture the retinol into the version your skin needs to be effective. The farther it is up the conversion chain, the less likely it will ever reach its target. The result is that your skin will get minimal repair of your dermal safety net. Refer to retinoids in your Skin Pearls Glossary.

The following products represent the newest retinol technology. Instead of two-to-four skin remanufacturing steps, the journey to reach its target is a much shorter one. In fact, in only one step, the retinol converts to the prescription retinoid deep inside your skin. It remanufactures itself into the most-powerful anti-wrinkle stimulator to date—a prescription retinoid. Trust me on this one.

This little miracle is called retinaldahyde. It is new and more expensive than other retinoids. Because of the expense and newness, it will be a while before the larger skincare companies catch up and incorporate it into their products. However, it is available now from a handful of skincare companies.

Glytone® Night Renewal Cream

Priced at physician offices.
Glytone-USA.com

A nighttime cream formulated with glycolic acid and retinaldehyde to help clarify, smooth, and firm skin, revealing younger, healthier-looking skin. Apply at night and avoid sun exposure. Available through certified physicians.

Avene Professional-RetinAL 0.1 Cream

$69.00 - *AveneUSA.com*

Contains retinaldehyde (although not in the stabilized form) clinically proven to be more effective than retinol. Also contains a pro-elastin peptide to help skin look firmer and plumper, along with powerful antioxidants.

BeautyProof® Dragōne D'Or Stimulating Serum

$ 87.00 - *BeautyProof.com*

Delivers deep, intensive wrinkle repair that equals or exceeds prescription-strength products. Wrinkles are regressed 50%, redness diminished by 70%. The first stable retinaldehyde in a non-irritating formula. True youth in a bottle.

"Fads are missed opportunities to create real changes in your skin."

FACE THE FADS

Here are a few of the latest fads. Alluring to the consumer—yes. Effective to repair wrinkles—no.

Plant Stem Cells Bottom line, these are powerful antioxidants. They nourish and protect your skin, but are unable to communicate with your skin cells in the same way human stem cells do. They just can't. Use these agents only for their "protective" qualities.

Neuronal Peptides These peptides claim to be Botox in a bottle. They inhibit the neurotransmitters responsible for muscle contraction, but only on an extremely superficial skin level. Investing in real Botox injections will save you the disappointment and will relax your wrinkles long enough for your repair agents to work. Argeline is a popular peptide in this category. It doesn't hurt to have this product included in your skincare—it will have a very subtle effect, but do nothing to repair your wrinkles.

Instant Wrinkle Reducers These agents plump up the dead cells on the skin surface and create a temporary smoothing effect—nothing more. Other formulations are applied wet and temporarily stretch the skin surface after they dry with a transparent film.

FACE THE FACTS

The longer you wait to repair your wrinkles, the more difficult it will become to reverse them later on. Remember that every day is an opportunity to help turn back the clock. When you choose to use only the fads, you miss out on the opportunities true science can bring. No one agent is a miracle cure, but you should try to at least include agents high on my stimulator efficacy scale found in the THE SYSTEM chapter. I've used the top stimulators along with my THE SYSTEM method for thirty years, and I wouldn't have it any other way.

SKIN SAVVY

- When does a wrinkle become a crease? Any day you choose to go without sunscreen, you sizzle away your youthful skin and set the stage for deep creases to develop. You've learned that UV rays cause tissue buildup that flank each wrinkle, giving you coarser, deeper, wider wrinkles—or in other words, creases.

- Purge your vanity of quick fixes—they waste your time, money, and ultimately create disappointment. The time you take applying your quick fixes could be used working with real repair agents that truly do reset the clock on your skin. See my interview with Dr. Schell which starts on page 90 of this book.

- Which products offer the most wrinkle repair? Products that get past the gatekeepers and reach the dermis, where wrinkles develop. Choose from a variety of 4 to 5 star wrinkle-repair agents listed in my stimulator chart on page 179.

- Some of the best wrinkle preventers are some of the least expensive. Don't smoke, avoid the sun, stop the sugar splurges, make an easy oil switch (in your kitchen not your garage), bump up the protein, and most of all, avoid spending big bucks on products with empty promises. More to come.

- If your cosmetic person swears that her moisturizer fixes wrinkles and tightens skin, then run!! News flash—moisturizers do nothing to repair wrinkles! Trust me on this one.

- Stay in the game longer by learning a little patience. You didn't get your wrinkles in a few days or a week. When you use the right actives, you need to first fire up the collagen factories (fibroblasts) and give them time to do their thing. Be patient. Your skin will thank you by standing the test of time!

LOSS OF FIRMNESS

FIRMNESS FACTOR #1

We've just learned that when experts examine wrinkles through high-tech methodology, they view a gap in the collagen network underneath each and every wrinkle. It is widely accepted that collagen depletion is the number-one culprit leading to wrinkle formation. But what changes in skin are responsible for the loss of firmness or the medical term elastosis? We notice our skin doesn't feel as tight. It doesn't snap back the way it did in our youth. This is due to a breakdown of a skin protein called elastin. Keep in mind that collagen is the protein that is responsible for the firmness in skin, while elastin is the protein that gives the skin stretch and flexibility. Elastin helps the skin to snap back after it is pinched or pulled. Collagen does have elastic properties, however it is elastin, that makes up only 3% of the dermis that provides the skin with what it needs to stretch and be flexible.

When your skin is in it's perfect state, it has small elastic fibers intermeshed among the collagen network. These fibers stretch somewhat like a rubber band. When you notice slackness in your skin, these fibers become scarce and are no longer evenly interwoven inside your safety net. This is due to a variety of factors such as sun, a diet lacking adequate amounts of protein, too much alcohol, and hormonal imbalance—especially in women. In fact, menopause is the number-one reason women lose the firmness of their youth.

There's another factor that makes the problem of elastosis go haywire, and that's the sun. Called actinic elastosis, it is a condition is unique to sun worshippers. When you see someone with yellowed, rough, and leathery-looking skin, you are seeing someone with this condition. Actinic elastosis is not an equal-opportunity ager. In fact, for sun worshipers, African Americans are the one group of people who seem to be mostly spared. Roughly 80% of sun-seeking Caucasians will suffer it, followed by 47% Latinos and 10% African Americans.

Let's have a look deep inside actinic elastosis. In a nutshell, elastin fibers hugely multiply in numbers and become tangled and non-functional. Like a ball of discarded and degraded rubber bands, they become useless in their ability to put the bounce in your skin. What's more, the discarded bundles of ineffective elastin make wrinkles deeper and more dramatic. The degraded material flanks a wrinkle and causes an increase in their magnitude.

But let's return to a general loss of firmness. While there are habits that can make general sagginess worse, like smoking, a diet lacking protein, or excess alcohol intake, even the healthiest of individuals may find themselves victims of this problem. Along with the THE SYSTEM: SMOOTH • STRENGTHEN • STIMULATE unique to your heritage, you'll read about supplements that protect skin from UV rays and others that help fuel and firm skin along with easy "add-ons" to any diet that give you the ageless advantage.

HEALTHY SKIN

In youthful tight skin there is an abundance of healthy elastic tissue, providing stretch and snap.

SLACK SKIN

Skin that lacks firmness has a deficit of the elastic network. Skin is unable to spring back when pulled or stretched.

FIRMNESS FACTOR #2

Did you know that the face has the biggest range of muscular structure in the human body? Your facial muscles are also the only ones in your entire body that attach directly to your skin. If you don't keep your facial muscles toned, over time they will slacken and become weak, limp, and unable to support the skin they are attached to. As a result, your face will lose volume and sag—no matter what condition your dermal-safety net-is in. This is one-third of the firmness factor you should address. By stimulating the underlying facial muscles that attach to your skin, you can add precious volume and recontour your face.

MULTIPLE BENEFITS

- Help keep your skin tight and firm.
- Help stimulate the production of collagen.
- Increase blood flow to your skin.
- Stimulate the lymphatic system that resides underneath the skin.

Patricia Goroway, Facial Fitness

$8.44 - *Amazon.com*

Unlike many facial exercise books, Patricia's are clear and simple to follow. Comes with an invaluable DVD and has high approval ratings from her readers.

Catherine Pez, The 5-Minute Facial Workout

$8.44 - *Amazon.com*

The benefit is that the 5-minute facial workout is the time factor. You can easily perform her exercises when you have a few spare minutes. Also ranked high for its ease of use and results.

Carole Maggio, Ultimate Facercise

$10.49 - *Amazon.com*

Commit to the longer 15-minute workout for two weeks, and then half the time to her 8-minute workout. My favorite. Find Carole on YouTube and see for yourself! Simply brilliant.

Reinhold Benz, Five Minute Face-lift

$8.45 - *Amazon.com*

Full color, step-by-step photos work on everything from your temples to the tip of your nose. Easy to follow, too! A small price to pay in time and money for a firmer, redefined face.

FIRMNESS FACTOR #3

Most specialists agree. Volume loss, not sagging skin, causes the loss of firmness you experience as the years pile up. In fact, they view this as the major component contributing to the development of smile or laugh lines around the mouth and nose (also known as nasolabial folds). Fat transfers are becoming increasingly popular because the results are natural and improve the skin's quality. Your fat contains a wealth of stem cells, and fat transfers are truly youthifying. Please refer to my interview with Dr. Kahn for more details.

What about fillers other than using your own fat? Alternative fillers are plentiful today, showing up not only in dermatologist and plastic surgery offices, but also in medispas and even your own general physician down the block from your local pharmacy. Everyone is embracing them! Patients are happy because they can recapture their youthful appearance, and doctors love having happy patients—along with the ongoing stream of revenue they generate. But there are differences in fillers—especially in lifting effects and lifespan. Bottom line, you should do your research on the pluses and minuses before you get your credit cards out.

First a little history lesson. Well over half a century ago, silicone fillers were invented. They quickly became the rage for everything from breast augmentation to facial wrinkles. But problems arose. Big problems. Some proponents of silicone injection claim that inexperienced hands and quality were the source of many of these problems, but despite these claims, the literature is replete with disastrous outcomes. After silicone fillers were essentially banned from the cosmetic industry, collagen fillers became the next big thing. Considered to be worlds safer than silicone, they were made from naturally occurring bovine collagen. But still problems developed, albeit not nearly as serious as was the case with silicone. Allergic reactions were a big concern. As a consequence, patients needed to be tested first. What's more, the collagen was quickly absorbed by the body, making the effect relatively short in duration.

Since then, better fillers have evolved and we will continue to see more in the future. While much safer and user friendly than fillers from the early days, there are important differences you should be aware of. A little knowledge can ensure you're getting the results you want—and your money's worth.

1. TEMPORARY

- Restylane ®
- Perlane ®
- Belotero ®
- Captique ®
- Juvéderm ®

Above are some of the most-popular hyaluronic acid fillers. Hyaluronic acid is a natural filler substance that is produced by the human body. Most of the differences in these products are due to particle size. Some, such as Belotero, are smaller, softer, more malleable, and are better suited for superficial lines and wrinkles. Deeper wrinkles—such as the grooves between the nose and lip area—are better treated with a hyaluronic acid with larger particle size, such as Perlane or Juvéderm Ultra Plus. Many of these fillers now contain added lidocaine to reduce pain as it is being injected into wrinkles. This class of hyaluronic fillers is temporary, and will typically last between six months to two years.

2. SEMI-PERMANENT

- Radiesse ®
- Sculptra ®

Products in this group are termed "stimulating fillers," because they contain substances that actually increase collagen content in your skin. In other words, instead of temporarily filling the hollow space, your dermal "safety net" is expanded, tightened, and thickened. These products can be injected more deeply and are considered superior to others for their volume generation and lifting effects. Radiesse gives an immediate filler effect lasting 1-2 years, while increasing natural collagen production over a period of time. Sculptra isn't immediate and requires multiple injections, but the results can be spectacular.

3. PERMANENT

- Artefill®

Artefill contains a synthetic ingredient mixed with animal-derived collagen. Usually it requires one-to-two injections to achieve desired results, and testing is required. It is more expensive than most fillers, but the end result is permanent and patients love it for its consistency over time. The only catch is you need to find a specialist skilled and trained specifically for this filler because, if injected improperly, lumping and nodules can occur.

SKIN SAVVY

It's not just about hot flashes! One of the biggest complaints of menopausal women is that their skin seems to lose all elasticity. Estrogen loss combined with sun exposure creates internal changes that makes loss of firmness accelerate at the speed of light. Menopause is an important period of a woman's life—a time when her aging vulnerability is greatly increased. Always use SPF 30 or above, rain or shine, no exceptions. An ounce of protection really is worth a pound of cure. Be ageless by making smart choices.

When more becomes less. We have just learned that slack skin is caused by a depletion in elastin levels. However, UV rays create an increase, not a decrease in elastin. The problem for sun worshippers is that the elastin does not make skin spring back. Instead, the increase is discarded as useless balls flanking wrinkles. Another double whammy!

You're never immune to loss of elasticity, no matter what your age! It usually starts around the mid-twenties, and you'll first see it in the area of the eyes. However, due to excessive lifestyle choices, slack skin can start as early as the late teens! If you are a crazy, out-of-control teen who loves to party, like I'm ashamed to say I was, rethink what your idea of fun is. Choosing fun over your face is no longer a joke when you suffer the consequences for the rest of your life.

Sudden weight loss can also be a factor when it comes to losing elasticity and firmness. Health experts advise slow but steady weight loss that incorporates adequate levels of protein. This ensures the rest of the body (including the skin) can keep up.

Yes, a lot of little changes all add up! Aside from the recommended products and ingredients you'll be reading about, is there more you can do to control slackness? Yes, there is...

• Partaking in regular exercise. A minimum of 30 minutes of regular exercise each day improves circulation and feeds skin.

• Eat the best proteins for good elasticity. Almonds, peanut butter, eggs, salmon, and sardines are all good choices.

• Try fish or krill oil capsules. Be sure to follow the dosage instructions since the wrong dose could be harmful or dangerous in bleeding disorders.

• There is evidence that lutein—found in egg yolks, spinach, and other leafy greens—may improve skin elasticity by as much as 20 percent. Incorporate spinach and daily greens in your protein smoothies.

REDNESS

Broken capillaries often becomes more prominent as you age because your skin gets thinner and it's easier to see them just under the surface. Fair-skinned people who are genetically prone to thinner skin are most often the ones who experience this condition. Broken capillaries, or as it is referred medically, telangiectasia, often first develops around the cheek and nasal area. It comes on gradually and then slowly spreads, often in lacy blotches throughout the cheeks, forehead, and even the chin. What you are seeing in the mirror are tiny malfunctioning, twisted, dilated capillaries with pooling of the blood just below the skin's surface. What causes them? Chronic inflammatory conditions are probably the prime offender. Outside of rosacea, an inflammatory condition, experts feel that sun is the number-one culprit. As you'll read ahead in Chapter 4, sun is an extremely potent driver of inflammation for your skin. Other reasons could be excessive irritation such as using harsh detergents or too many aggressive facial peels. Another factor to think about is too many drinks on too many nights. Excessive drinking of alcohol over a long period of time can increase your blood pressure, causing the veins on your face to di-

late. It becomes permanent when repeated dilation tends to lock the veins in that position. Like so much else in life, moderation is key. Spider veins are just another negative consequence of too much alcohol.

The bad news is that once the vessel walls are broken, they cannot be reversed by topical or oral medications to any significant degree. Damaged capillaries will not constrict back to their normal thickness or repair themselves.

SPIDER VEINS

It's never too late...

To repair the damage. If you suffer from broken blood vessels or pooled capillaries, they can be repaired with the latest laser treatments. But it's not a one-size-fits-all approach. Depending on ethnic background, the type of damage, and body location, some lasers are superior in performance than others.

Before making any appointments, there are two rules you should first consider.

RULE #1

Your redness needs to be properly diagnosed by a specialist. Please don't count on your family practitioner, or your local esthetician—or worse still, that person behind the cosmetic counter. For example, your spider veins could be due to a condition called rosacea. Rosacea is often misdiagnosed—even by primary care physicians who are not specifically trained in dermatology. Many people don't realize that rosacea can be corrected by prescription creams and antibiotics.

RULE #2

You need to ensure you're getting the laser that's most effective. Some offices are equipped with only one laser machine, and they will try to make it "fit," even though it may not be the best option for you. While IPL (intense pulsed light) is considered the gold standard for redness, some specialists do not find it as effective for treating telangiectasia or dilated, pooled small blood vessels as some other lasers. PDLs (pulsed dye lasers) such as Versa-Pulse, V-Star, or an Nd:YAG may be better options for you.

Lasers may also be an effective treatment for leg veins, but only if the veins are too small to be treated by injection.

Bottom line: Seek out a dermatologist who specializes in lasers, and who has more than one at his disposal. One to three sessions are usually required to achieve ideal outcomes.

ROSACEA

Believe it or not, 1 in every 20 Americans—14 million people—are believed by researchers to be affected with some form of rosacea. Even so, a Gallup survey revealed that almost 80 percent of Americans do not know anything about this skin condition.

If you suspect rosacea, please do not rely on any-one except a dermatologist to assess your condi-tion. It is commonly misdiagnosed as acne, general hypersensitivity, eczema, or some other skin allergy. During your exam, you should explain any problems you are having, such as redness, the appearance of bumps or pimples, swelling, burning, itching, or stinging. Early treatment is critical as this condition worsens if left undiagnosed and untreated.

WHAT CAUSES IT?

Although the exact cause of rosacea is unknown, various theories have developed over the years. Here are a few:

1. Facial capillaries dilate in a hair-trigger fashion. The increased blood near the skin's surface makes the skin appear flushed and red.

2. Environmental and lifestyle triggers can immedi-ately increase this redness response.

3. Tiny acne-like bumps may appear in the red areas of your face. These bumps may be related to skin bacteria, irritation of the follicles, sun damage, and an abnormal immune (inflammatory) response.

ARE TREATMENTS EFFECTIVE?

In the past, skincare has effectively treated only the least-severe subtypes of rosacea. Recent advances into the understanding of this skin condition have resulted in more-effective agents that work across multiple pathways. They go beyond symptom con-trol, and are actually beginning to have an impact on the disease itself. Here are some of today's most-ef-fective treatment options:

1. Anti-inflammatories and antioxidants such as licorice extract and green tea reduce inflammation.

2. Barrier-repair moisturizers strengthen the stratum corneum and reduce skin susceptibility to external irritants.

3. Actives such as centella asiatica (gotu kola) reduce vascular permeability and help strengthen capillaries.

4. Prescription antibiotics are highly effective in some cases.

5. Vasoconstrictors can immediately diminish facial redness.

Bottom line: If you suspect this condition, make an appointment with your dermatologist.

SKIN SAVVY

When your skin has a redness problem, it can some-times come flaring in—aggressive and angry—or it can just be a hypersensitivity issue. Getting to the underlying problem will save you the time and ex-pense of slathering on the green and yellow primers and powders to camouflage the problem. Instead of using quick fixes, get to the root of the problem. A little know-how and knowledge can go a long way.

Here are a few rules to follow…

• Forget the hot showers—lukewarm water won't aggravate your capillaries nearly as much.

• Alcohol? One drink max. Who wants to look like a lush anyway?

• You can't change mother nature, but try to stay in an air-conditioned environment during the day. For most of us, that's easy—it's called having a job. Indoors, of course.

Whether or not your redness is due to dilated, bro-ken capillaries, rosacea, hypersensitive skin, and so forth, here are a few things to avoid…

• Anything with alcohol in it, which means most toners. Oh well, they do nothing to combat aging anyway!

• Fragrances or any product that stings your skin. Sorry about that fragrance lovers!

• Chemical sunscreens. Always opt for going natural with zinc oxide or titanium dioxide. Nothing's worse than slathering on a chemical sunscreen and then enduring a burning, stinging feeling!

• Cleansers containing sulfates. Avoid these at all costs. Reasonably priced sulfate-free cleansers can be found at your local pharmacy. Just ask your pharmacist for help.

• Avoid all glycolic acids, salicylic acids, and reti-nols. But don't worry, there are many other non-sen-sitizing wrinkle-repair products available.

What type of anti-ager should you look for? Your best anti-ager would be a proven peptide, such as Matrixyl® synthe. It's non irritating with a wealth of collagen-building evidence. Growth factors are a good second choice, though they are more expen-sive.

How do I exfoliate my skin if cleansing grains are a no-no, you may ask? Products containing gentle fruit acids are a good option. Just remember to be extra careful and start by applying only once weekly.

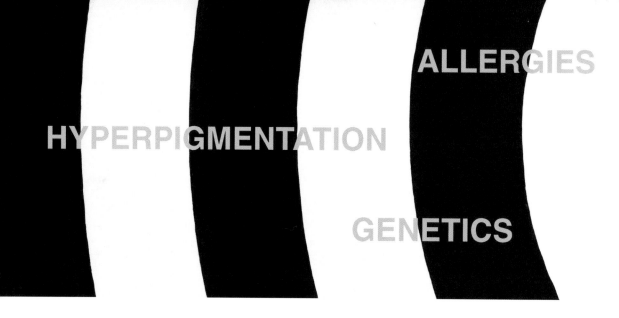

DARK CIRCLES

Dark circles affect a vast majority of the population, and many of us have experienced them much more than we'd like from such things as lack of sleep, too many nights out partying, or out-of-control hay fever. Then there are the circles that appear darkish brown, the ones that never seem to go away. Besides wrinkles, most of us feel that nothing is more unsightly than dark circles. Not only do they seem to make people look tired, dark circles make them look much older than they really are.

THE CONFUSION WE FACE

One of the many reasons why unrelenting dark circles are so frustrating for women and men is that we are given such conflicting explanations for why they come about and how to treat them. We are told various reasons—that they are hereditary, that they

are an inconsequential result of aging, or that they are a result of a hormonal or iron deficiency. We attempt to get more sleep, eat a better diet, and take supplements, but the circles don't seem to fade. It's confusing to hear each person's theory and solution on dark circles and not knowing when and if any of these treatments will have any luck. Surprisingly, the causes and solutions can be broken down and understood, and what's more, modern technology has given us treatments that can correct even the most stubborn raccoon eyes.

2 STUBBORN REASONS, LET'S TALK

First, let's talk about the more-permanent kind of dark circles. Although there may be overlap, there are two separate changes happening inside our skin that causes these. The first is due to thinning skin with impaired

blood supply, and the other is a result of our skin producing too much pigment or melanin. Hyperpigmentation, which is basically too much melanin in the skin, is more common in people from Asia, Africa, Southern Italy, and the Middle East. While genetics can be a factor in causing this disorder, sun exposure and inflammation can also add to the skin's darkening.

WHAT'S CAUSING YOURS?

How can you tell if this is what you are suffering from? One way that dermatologists determine if hyperpigmentation is the cause of dark circles is by gently pressing a finger over the circle and then releasing it. If the skin remains dark, you are most likely suffering from an overproduction of melanin. In addition, if one of your parents has constant dark circles, you are more likely to get them, as they are hereditary.

GENETICS

Treating dark circles under the eyes caused by hyperpigmentation usually requires help from a physician. Of course, dark circles can be temporarily hidden with the use of a concealer, but this is just a quick fix and ultimately not a long-term solution. A physician may attempt to treat your circles with a prescription-strength hydroquinone skin whitener that is considered to be the gold standard of all skin whiteners. While this may be an effective way to treat dark circles, there are risks involved with its use, such as black spots appearing on the skin after prolonged use. Not only that, but skin whiteners have been banned in Europe because they have been linked to certain types of cancers. Hydroquinone is available in over-the-counter formulations, but please refer to your Skin Pearls Glossary for more information.

If topical treatments prove ineffective, your physician may recommend laser treatment. This is where you, as the consumer, need to do some investigation in order to protect yourself. There are many types of lasers out there, and a physician will usually offer treatments using one or two of them. The problem with laser treatment is that it can actually darken the skin instead of correcting the discoloration. To prevent this from happening, your physician should first treat a part of your skin that is normally hidden as a test. If there is no discoloration or darkening, then you know it is safe to proceed. One of the most-effective lasers for this condition is known as the Q-switched ruby laser. This specialized laser targets only specific areas of the skin, allowing the laser to effectively remove the excess pigment without causing any scarring. This is especially important in the fragile skin area

around the eyes. Another good option is the intense pulsed light (IPL) laser that you read about in the Broken Capillaries section of this book. Keep in mind that several laser treatments are usually needed to be beneficial.

The good news is that because the eye area is such a small space to treat, these treatments are pretty affordable for the average person. It's extremely important in the prevention of dark circles, and for your skin's overall health, to always use a high UV-protection sunscreen every day, rain or shine! Keep sunscreen by your toothbrush so that daily application becomes second nature. If you are prone to dark circles, remember that it doesn't take much sun for your old and unwanted friends, the raccoon eyes, to return, so be careful!

WHEN FILLERS MAY HELP

There is a second type of permanent dark circles under the eyes that are more bluish-reddish in appearance. Instead of being caused by an over-abundance of melanin, these particular circles are due to thinning of the skin and a pooling of blood in the capillaries beneath. As we age, we lose a fair amount of collagen and elastin, which causes the delicate skin around our eyes to begin to droop and cast a shadowy and darkened appearance. As we age, the fat around our eyes thins and gives the eyes a more hollowed look. This thinning of the skin makes the pooled area of dilated capillaries below the eye more visible, contributing to the discolored skin appearance around our eyes.

THE PERFECT COCKTAIL

There are various treatments for dark circles, and some are much more effective than others, it's just a matter of being properly informed! At the top of your list should be products that stimulate the skin to produce more of what keeps it young: collagen and elastin. Peptides have become a highly sought-after treatment as they are gentle yet effective, and a product containing soy peptides would be an excellent choice. Growth factors encourage a denser and firmer eye area, while antioxidants will help strengthen the cells and prevent further damage. You may encounter products with caffeine and other stimulants designed to encourage blood flow and flush out the pooled capillaries. You may choose to use these in conjunction with your skin-building peptide creams, but they don't work well alone.

Temporary dark circles may also be a problem, and they are caused by a number of different issues. Eye medications, particularly eye drops used to lower blood pressure in people suffering from glaucoma, can sometimes cause darkening of the surrounding skin. Allergies cause inflammation that can enlarge the tiny blood vessels below the eyes, and these swollen blood vessels press against the thin under-eye skin, leading to a darker color leaking through. An over-the-counter antihistamine will often solve this problem, treating the allergies while lessening the circles. Blocked nasal passages can also cause dark circles because the veins from the eyes to the nose become dilated and darken the skin below the eyes. Investing in a neti pot, which sends a saline solution of water and sea salt through your nasal passages, is a very effective and simple solution for this kind of problem.

Above all, it's important to make sure that you are enjoying a healthy diet and lifestyle. Drink plenty of water, as dehydration can cause the capillaries underneath your eyes to become swollen and dilated. And last of all, if someone tells you that you simply look tired, perhaps you are one of the lucky ones, and a good night's sleep will cure your problem!

RECOMMENDATIONS

LOOK FOR INGREDIENTS THAT:

Bump up Circulation – One reason bags and circles appear are due to lack of circulation in the eye area. Anything that speeds up circulation will flush out blood pigments that encourage discoloration.

Reduces Inflammation – You'll learn in the INFLAMMATION CHAPTER how a cascade of events can cause capillaries to dilate and leak.

Thicken Skin – The stronger your dermal collagen network the firmer your under eye skin and firm skin means less bags.

Heal Skin Barrier – When your epidermal layer is strong and healthy, your skin, can maintain moisture levels that are critical in this fragile area.

Clinique™ Even Better Eyes Dark Circle Corrector.

$39.50 - *Clinique.com*

Oil free formula strengthens delicate skin and visibly lightens dark circles by 30% in 12 weeks.. Uses "cooling" help break up puffiness.

Algenist® Complete Eye Renewal Balm

$65.00 - *Algenist.com*

A rich yet lightweight balm that includes a powerful bio active compound alguronic acid to fight visible signs of aging. The ingredient alguronic acid regenerates cells and increases elastin.

Perricone MD® Acyl-Glutathione Eye Lid Serum

$115.00 - *Perricone.com*

Scientifically formulated to firm the upper eye area and minimize the look of redness and dark circles. Enriched with Acyl-Glutathione, well known for its powerful antioxidant capabilities.

Claudalie ® Premier Cru The Eye Cream

$99.00 - *Claudalie USA.com*

A luxurious cream that hydrates, lightens and firms. Dark circles and puffiness fade away with the inclusion of three highly concentrated plant-based antioxidants.

BeautyProof ® Go Glow Eyes

$55.00 - *BeautyProof.com*

Designed for even the most delicate eye area. Redness is soothed and healed while under-eye darkness is brightened due to the melanin inhibition factors. Skin is firmed, plumped, and nourished.

SKIN SAVVY

Dark circles under eyes are a surefire way to look older, tired, and even ill. Here are a few tips about dark circles resulting from lifestyle, allergies, thin skin, and collagen loss.

- As collagen decreases with age, skin becomes more translucent. Peptides—and the newest, most-effective retinol without a prescription, retinaldehyde—are good bets to rev up your collagen factories.

- Nutrition really counts. Your tiny capillaries weaken over time and blood pools as the veins dilate. Ensure you're on a high-protein diet with an abundant amount of veggies and low-sugar fruits. Vitamin K has mixed reviews but is worth a try.

- A lack of sleep can make veins dilate too. Get your ZZZs! Ensure you're not sabotaging your beauty sleep by drinking alcohol before bed. Lack of sleep also makes the rest of your skin paler and makes the dilated blood vessels more obvious!

- Speaking of alcohol, the combination of salt and alcohol leads to noticeable water retention. A bloated face creates deeper circles that no amount of makeup can fix!

- If you tend to wake up with puffy eyes, sleep on an extra pillow to help drain excess fluid throughout the night. If you still have puffiness when you awaken, try using a cold compress or refrigerated cucumber slices. Give each 10 to 15 minutes to work while you listen to your morning news.

- If your puffiness is due to fat pads, only a visit to a plastic surgeon can fix the problem. Expensive, yes, but you'll probably be happy you unloaded your pocketbook!

- Many dark circles are caused by allergies. Of course, avoidance of the offending allergen is your first choice. If you can't avoid it, try over-the-counter or prescription medications. Investing in a neti pot may help.

- People with allergies tend to be deficient in vitamin B6, folic acid, and vitamin B12, or your allergies could be an intolerance to gluten. If your allergies are negatively impacting your life, an allergist is well worth the time and expense.

If your dark circles are hereditary and the result of an overproduction in melanin, you need to see a dermatologist who is experienced in the arena of hyperpigmentation. Ask around, and seek out recommendations from others who have the same issue. Please read my interview with Dr. Wendy Roberts on page 126. She provides a wealth of information as she is one of the leading experts in the United States.

That said, here are a few more tips.

* Avoid rubbing or scratching your eye area, no matter how you may feel! Something as simple as a rub or scratch can set off a cascade of melanin, making your dark circles even darker.

* Absolutely do not even think of using illegal skin lighteners. I've seen photos of the horrible consequences these treatments can bring. You would be absolutely shocked, not to mention saddened, that anyone could suffer such a fate. There is a good reason these treatments are illegal.

* Dark circles caused by hyperpigmentation are usually experienced by people of color. Lasers can be effective, but must be conducted by a physician skilled in this field. In the wrong hands, the dark circles could become darker.

* Fillers have been receiving good reviews, even for circles caused by melanin overdrive. A trial of Restylane® or another temporary filler is a good first choice. If you like the results, consider a fat transfer or Artefill® which will last much longer.

DARK SPOTS

Whatever your skin tone may be, most of us want our skin to appear even-toned and flawless. A luminous and even complexion truly is a thing of beauty. At its most youthful, African American skin has one of the most luminous qualities of all skin, Asian skin is reminiscent of a perfect pearl, and Caucasian skin has a rosy glow to it. But what happens to everyone as they get older, and where does that even, translucent quality in their skin go? It seems that the older we get, the more we find ourselves searching for the perfect foundations that promise to capture the even glow we enjoyed in our youth. In this section, we will uncover what happens deep inside your skin that causes the mottled appearance that may add at least a decade to your appearance.

Most of the unevenness that we see in the mirror is due to melanin produced naturally in our skin. The role of melanin is to absorb and scatter energy from ultraviolet light to protect the epidermal cells from damage. Melanin is the pigment in the cells that protect the skin from the sun, and this pigment enables darker-skinned people, particularly African Americans, to hang onto a youthful appearance much longer than Western Europeans. In fact, research tells us that 55 percent of UV rays penetrate Caucasian skin, while fewer than 18 percent of UV rays penetrate African American skin.

The majority of people around the world are born with the same number of cells that are capable of producing melanin, called melanocytes. It is the differences in production and distribution of melanin that mark the differences in the ethnicities. The dark-er your skin, the greater the distribution of melanin into the skin cells. Types of melanin also create differences in tonality—Asians produce a golden type of melanin called phaeomelanin and black skin produces an ebony colored and thicker melanin called eumelanin.

CUMULATIVE DAMAGE

Brown spots and discoloration in the skin happen on a cellular level. Age spots, liver spots, or lentigines (as they are referred to in the medical community) usually crop up in faired-skinned individuals after 20 to 30 years of cumulative sun damage. The melanin-producing cells in fair-skinned individuals become highly erratic, and the melanin is distributed in concentrated clusters instead of evenly. As for sun exposure, the key word here is *cumulative*—the development of brown spots and discolorations are not directly related to any single sunburn on any specific day.

Without a doubt, prevention is key. Using a broad-spectrum sunscreen, preferably one with zinc oxide, will stop the development of age spots in its tracks. The good news is that if it's too late for you to prevent these age spots, you're not entirely out of luck. Unlike wrinkles, age spots and discoloration affect the outermost layer of the skin, so there are several treatment options to get rid of them. Like spilling coffee on a pad of paper, if you peel away the paper one sheet at a time, you will eventually get rid of the stain. Refer to the skin lighteners in the Skin Pearls Glossary to understand the effects of the various agents.

DARK SPOTS REVEALED

There is another form of dark, blotchy unevenness that can appear on your skin as a result of something as simple as using the wrong cleanser or trying an anti-aging approach that is too aggressive. This is called hyperpigmentation. Like age spots in faired-skinned individuals, hyperpigmentation is when melanin production becomes disorganized, erratic, and out-of-control. This condition happens in people of African American, Indian, and Asian heritage, and although this group of people age much better than Western Europeans, what keeps them young can also be a recipe for a discolored and uneven complexion without proper care. Any ingredient that has the potential to cause significant irritation or dryness when applied to the skin can cause pigment alteration in these ethnicities.

Although hypopigmentation—loss of pigment—can also occur, hyperpigmentation is more common. The population that is at greatest risk for hypopigmentation includes darker-skinned individuals with sensitive and dry skin. The most common treatments associated with developing this condition include benzoyl peroxide, retinoids, salicylic acid, and glycolic acid. Typically, dark-skinned individuals experience dryness and irritation, followed by uneven patches of skin darkening. Experts have found that these effects can be mitigated if the anti-agers, such as glycolic and salicylic acid, are incorporated into an emollient base. A highly effective moisturizer is also a must have, and moisturizers containing lactic acid have proven effective against hyperpigmentation. Don't worry if these treatments aren't right for you. If dark spots don't seem to budge after a trial of various skin lighteners, simply seek out a dermatologist who is equipped with lasers such as the Q-switched ruby laser to address the issue. Remember, your skin is highly sensitive, so make sure a skin test takes place on a less-visible part of your skin before proceeding with any treatment.

RECOMMENDATIONS

THREE'S NOT A CROWD!

When you're serious about correcting dark spots or uneven discoloration, you need to do these three specific things to your skin.

1. Stop fueling your skin's dark-spot factories. Just like adding gasoline to a lit flame, any time your skin faces UV rays unprotected, you ignite the process that leads to uneven skin tone.

2. Don't depend on a single ingredient to shortcircuit the dark-spot process. Each corrector works in its own unique way. If you combine multiple correctors, you attack the development of spots on multiple fronts. The more the merrier!

3. Get past the gatekeepers. A gatekeeper is the buildup of dead cells that occurs if you don't embrace smoothing or exfoliating on a daily basis. When you allow the buildup to increase, it becomes much more difficult for your correctors to penetrate and go to work. Yes—there are now skin-smoothing techniques that are not only effective, but gentle!

"Following a few rules will go a long way to getting your glow on!"

Dior, Diorsnow Anti-Spot Serum

$150.00 - *Dior.com*

This formula is enriched with Icelandic glacial water and purified mallow extract providing strong anti-spot action. After just four weeks of use, women claimed the intensity of their dark spots reduced by 25 percent.

Peter Thomas Roth, De-Spot™ Plus

$78.00 - *Sephora.com*

This lightening treatment contains hydroquinone, the gold standard for spot correction. It also features three other correctors that brighten as well as prevent the skin-damaging effects of ultraviolet radiation.

Kate Somerville
LumiWhite™ Dark Spot Corrector

$55.00 - *KateSomerville.com*

A perfect choice for those who seek a hydroquinone-free spot corrector. Visibly diminishes the appearance of discoloration with a blend of natural ingredients.

Radical Skincare™
Multi Brightening Serum

$150.00 - *Skincare.com*

Uses multiple extracts such as brown algae and sea lily to inhibit melanin transfer and production. Also includes a natural exfoliant to accelerate spot reduction.

BeautyProof® Flash Focus Spot Corrector

$78.00 - *BeautyProof.com*

A remarkable serum delivering extraordinary lightening and fading effects. Uses a revolutionary high level of actives that work in tandem to give you dramatic spot reduction. Includes the gold standard, hydroquinone, combined with five other lightening actives. Results seen in 10 days use.

SKIN SAVVY

When it comes to skin aging, genetics matter. We all encounter pluses and minuses. If you are of African, Asian, or Latino descent, you will most likely remain decades younger looking than your European sisters. But, unfortunately, many women of color are prone to developing a type of inflammatory disorder called post-inflammatory hyperpigmentation. In plain English, you have a good chance of developing dark spots or other bothersome forms of discoloration as you age.

Skin prone to developing dark spots is like a powder keg waiting to explode. When a spark sets off the development of a dark spot, it can last from weeks to months to years. A hyper-reactive explosion in skin means your melanin cells are going haywire. Any type of spark—like a pimple, scratch, insect bite or even blackhead extraction—means it's time to find that concealer and pray this one won't hang around too long.

When it comes to dark spots, there's a lot of focus on how to get rid of them, but not much on how to avoid them in the first place. Dark spots are preventable—remember, an ounce of prevention is worth a pound of cure. Here are a few things to avoid...

• Avoid squeezing or popping a pimple.

• Never pick at a scab.

• As soon as you see a pimple, apply benzoyl peroxide twice a day. The longer a pimple remains, the darker the spot.

• Better yet, start using benzoyl peroxide every day to prevent pimples in the first place. If you find that this is too irritating, invest in products such as Proactive® that are gentler to skin, but still contain an effective level of benzoyl peroxide.

• Never apply a hot towel to a pimple, but do feel free to apply ice. Ice will help prevent inflammation from spreading.

Now let's touch on what medications could play a role in the development of your dark spots. Many African American and Latino women take medications for hypertension, diabetes, and heart disease. Red, itchy rashes can occur, leaving dark marks after they fade. Here are a few to watch out for...

• Antibiotics such as penicillin.

• Antihypertensives such as some ACE inhibitors and diuretics.

• Some type 2 diabetes drugs intended to control blood sugar levels.

Other drugs are known to cause a reaction when your skin is exposed to the sun. Always wear a hat, long sleeves, and use a broad-spectrum SPF. These reactions can happen to us all. Here are some of the worst offenders...

• Non-steroidal anti-inflammatory drugs such as naproxen. How common is that?

• Anti-yeast medications such as nystatin. Yes, we've all been there!

• Aspirin and some migraine meds. Ouch!

• Antibiotics—tetracycline is a biggie. Watch out.

• Oral contraceptives. Believe me on this one!

What about anti-agers, you may ask. Are they gentle enough? A good choice for your power-packed anti-ager would be peptides. These are gentle, kind to your skin, and pack powerful anti-aging, wrinkle-repair, and firming properties.

Lasers have evolved and are extremely effective in eliminating dark spots. If the price tag seems too high, remember that you will be saving time and money in concealers, not to mention the emotional burden and embarrassment dark spots, like acne, can create. You're worth starting a savings account for your self-esteem and beauty!

Not using an SPF of 30 or higher every day is like giving an open invitation for these troublesome pests to reappear. Even if they seem gone for good, any sunlight that hits the area where dark spots once appeared triggers your melanin to go into overdrive once again. Your skin remembers!

DRY SKIN AN AGING FACTOR OR A HEALTH CONCERN? READ ON...

Dry skin is something that the majority of us try to control daily, and after many a trial and error, we have found that special moisturizer that seems to get rid of the dryness and give our skin a nice moist and dewy appearance. Like a bottle of youth, super-soft skin seems within our reach. But just how much does a good moisturizer help slow the aging clock? Do moisturizers actually prevent and treat what most of us fear most—lines and wrinkles?

DO MOISTURIZERS GUARD AGAINST WRINKLES?

The evidence is overwhelming that while moisturizers help prevent dryness, bruising, and tearing, they have no effect on wrinkles themselves. Wrinkles are caused by a breakdown of collagen production—remember, collagen is the protein that gives your skin its plumpness and firmness. When collagen breaks down, we begin to see wrinkles,

and the only way to stop this is to increase the production of collagen.

Cosmetic manufacturers make a large amount of money from their dry skin lines of products, largely claiming that if dry skin is left untreated, it will lead to wrinkles. While extremely superficial lines can be caused by lack of skin hydration, moisturizers can only temporarily fix the problem by plumping up the stratum corneum. Wrinkles, on the other hand, are caused by sun damage, a sugary diet, and menopause. The only proven way to improve and prevent wrinkles is through prescription retinoids, alpha-hydroxy acids, growth factors, peptides, and retinaldehyde.

WHAT MOISTURIZERS REALLY DO?

But if moisturizers cannot prevent or repair wrinkles, what is their role in age prevention? First of all, we should be aware that moisturizers are only treating the

outermost layer of the skin—the stratum corneum, which is the dead and hardened cell layer that is visible to the eye. The moisture content of the stratum corneum is only about 15 percent. The water content increases the deeper you go into the dermis, to about 80 percent. As you can see, the water content inside the skin is much higher than it is in the very top layer that is exposed to the air. Therefore, in the absence of a barrier, water is much more likely to leave the skin. In a perfect world, skin produces enough lipids to maintain an effective barrier and keep from losing water and becoming dry. But, in reality, everyday irritants such as harsh soaps and cleansers containing sulfates that can upset the skin's natural balance by removing the protective lipids.

Another problem with dryness is that it impairs desquamation, which is the skin's built-in mechanism for renewing itself. Desquamation is when the dead and hardened skin cells break

their glue-like bond so that they can be easily sloughed off, and younger cells can migrate to the surface. Your skin has a built-in enzyme system that makes this vital process possible, but the catch is that the enzymes need the natural lipids to survive and do their work. Dry skin self-perpetuates as a hardened blanket of very old cells that build up on the surface of the skin, making it even more difficult for moisturizers to do their work. So you can see how a moisturizer helps keep everything moving and healthy, but it will not prevent or repair wrinkles.

DO SOME PEOPLE NEED MOISTURIZERS MORE THAN OTHERS?

Most everyone who has suffered from dry skin needs a moisturizer and they also need to apply it right after bathing or cleansing to lock in the water content. But there's another group of people who may need a moisturizer for other reasons. In the case of

Asian, African American, and East Indian women, another important role of moisturizers is to help keep their skin in as healthy a state as possible. Many women and men with these ethnic backgrounds have skin that is extremely reactive and inflammatory, and this type of skin can easily become discolored by a process called hyperpigmentation. Just squeezing a blackhead, or a light scrape or bump, can send their melanin-producing cells into overdrive. The slightest adjustment to the skin causes an inflammatory cascade with the end result being dark, uneven spots and blotchiness. Maintaining a healthy barrier function is vital to these ethnicities, and utilizing a good moisturizer is key.

Another concern related to dryness for people of African American heritage is the development of an ashy complexion. There have been numerous studies that show that African American skin has a more compact outer layer of skin. This is both a blessing

and a curse as it is what gives their skin such a beautiful luminous quality due to their outermost layer being more compact, which allows light to reflect off the skin beautifully. But the flip side of this—the curse—is that their skin can almost overnight appear less luminous with an ashy tone. This appearance is ultimately due to the buildup of dehydrated and dead skin cells. One reason cells build up is because the dryness causes a breakdown of the natural desquamation process. Interestingly enough, moisturizers containing lactic acid have proven to be beneficial to people of Asian, African American, and East Indian heritage. In the past, it was believed that acids such as lactic acids disrupted the barrier function, leaving skin in a sensitized and reactive state. However, tests have demonstrated that lactic acid not only helps prevent water loss, but it can improve reactivity and increase resistance to irritation.

RECOMMENDATIONS

Dry skin can rear its ugly head in the form of rough-ness, scaling, flakiness, and even itchiness for each and every one of us—especially as we get older. As we age, our skin gets thinner and more fragile due to hormonal changes, a diet short of protein, and too much sugar consumption. When this happens, we have less of a protective barrier to inhibit mois-ture loss from our skin cells. Scientists call this the "barrier function." As a result, older skin becomes more vulnerable to the entrance of irritants and other culprits.

A NEW TYPE OF MOISTURIZER

With more insight into the importance of maintain-ing a healthy barrier function that protects our skin from the entrance of irritants and bacteria that could initiate and perpetuate a damaging inflammatory cascade, a new class of moisturizers has arrived on the scene. As you shop for moisturizers, you'll notice that many now have the wording "barrier repair" in their title. These new skin barrier repair creams aim to replenish the normal constituents of the intracellu-lar lipids and try to "fix" the epidermal barrier.

Another way of putting it is that these creams close-ly mimic your skin's own lipids that help cement cells together and form a barrier that protects your skin from the environment. Your skin's mix of intracellular lipids contain ceramides, fatty acids, and cholester-ol. Some research indicates that these lipids, when formulated in a facial cream, are so close to your skin's own mix that they are physically incorporated into your keratinocytes, or outer skin cells, and then are excreted back into the intracellular space to fix the brick wall mortar.

These creams are highly effective and an import-ant discovery for the average aging baby boomer who has noticed more dryness and reactivity to their skin as the years pile on. I still recommend the anti-agers outlined in my THE SYSTEM: SMOOTH • STRENGTHEN • STIMULATE chapter to be used under these highly effective, newer-generation moisture creams.

USE MORE OF THESE

Dermatologica® Barrier Repair

$42.00 - *Dermatologica.com*

A waterless moisturizer contains oat and botanical actives that work below the surface to interrupt inflammatory triggers that lead to sensitization.

CeraVe® Moisture Cream

$15.00 - *Cerave.com*

Unique because of it's delivery technology that provides controlled release of ceramides and other skin-nuturing ingredients throughout the day.

Epionce® Renewal Facial Cream

$94.00 - *Epionce.com*

This clinically proven cream hydrates skin while effectively stimulating barrier repair and reversing/preventing release of destructive inflammatory factors.

Osmotics Cosmaceuticals Cream Extreme Intensive Repair

$120.00 - *Osmotics.com*

This cream dramatically improves moisture retention, while alleviating dryness and irritation. Antioxidants and vitamins nourish while epidermal lipids repair skin's barrier.

BeautyProof ® Advanced Recovery Complex

$94.00 - *BeautyProof.com*

Ideal for any skin that is sensitized or environmentally challenged. So effective it can be used to accelerate the healing process following resurfacing procedures. Restores and fortifies skin's outer barrier.

USE LESS OF THESE

Skin is your body's largest organ, and it plays a large role in your overall health. Skin both absorbs and excretes nutrients as well as toxins through the pores. Anything our skin absorbs has the opportunity to potentially enter our bloodstream and become integrated into the body tissue. As a result, the list of ingredients to avoid is a lengthy one and would consume an entire chapter—and a boring one at that. Many synthetic ingredients, and even some natural ones found in health food stores, have links to some form of toxicity.

Please don't focus too much on what a product doesn't contain to the extent that you lose focus on what a product does do to control aging.

LOOK FOR PRODUCTS FREE OF

Parabens. Used as a preservative to inhibit microbial growth and extend shelf life. Preliminary research found parabens in breast cancer tumors.

Diazolidinyl urea. Imidazolidinyl urea. Often used as a preservative, the American Academy of Dermatology has found these chemicals to be a primary cause of contact dermatitis. Both chemicals release formaldehyde, which can be toxic.

Synthetic colors. Look for labels **FD&C** or **D&C** followed by a number. These make products look lovely, but can be carcinogenic.

Synthetic fragrance. Labeled simply as "fragrance," there is no way to tell what chemicals are actually used in the product. Some people may experience hyperpigmentation as the synthetic fragrance sets off an inflammatory cascade, resulting in brown spots and discoloration.

YOU CAN RELAX

The following ingredients have gotten a bad rap over the years. You just don't need to worry about these.

Alcohol. There are many types of alcohol, with some that can do incredibly good things for your skin. Ethanol, for example, is a topical penetration enhancer. It can pull or drag anti-aging compounds deeper into your skin. It is often used in pharmaceutical transdermal patches. These products are void of the much higher levels found in mouthwashes and hand sanitizers. Naturally, you want to keep any household ethanol products away from children. Fatty alcohols, cetyl alcohol, and stearyl alcohol are benign and used as thickeners in skin-care products.

Waxes. Vegetable and other waxes such as beeswax have also gotten bad press over the years. Skincare experts sometimes assume that they can clog pores and irritate skin. While they are inappropriate for anyone suffering from acne, the same as most other moisturizers, they contain emollient, soothing, and softening properties that helps dry skin retain moisture.

Petrolatum. Similar to waxes, some specialists warn that petroleum jelly can clog pores. The truth is that petroleum jelly such as good old Vaseline® is a very effective occlusive agent, which guards your skin from moisture loss. It also has remarkable skin-healing properties from cuts, scrapes, and scratches. While there's nothing exotic about a byproduct from oil wells, any medical textbook will state that's the product is undeniably effective and inexpensive.

But problems have arisen from inadequate and unsafe distilling processes. Because petroleum is derived from oil, it needs to be refined, and some methods for this refining have been shown to contain hazardous, toxic compounds. One of them, PHAs, have been linked to cancer. The bottom line is that petroleum jelly is not itself carcinogenic—never has been, and never will be if handled properly. If you want an effective and inexpensive moisturizer, go with a branded product like Vaseline®. It has been around for more than a hundred years, and has protected many baby bottoms over the years. Not only that, but it can be readily found in most medicine chests.

SKIN SAVVY

• There are many things that can alleviate dry skin, whether it's seasonal or persists year 'round. Below are some tips that can bring much-needed relief for this problem we all suffer from sooner or later.

• Hurray for modern science! Use a moisturizer in the Barrier Repair category (see page 73). These products create a healthier outer-skin layer that can hold moisture in better than average moisturizers. A healthy skin barrier means more moisture is captured below.

• Don't wait! Apply moisturizer to skin soon after cleansing and applying your serum. This will ensure vital moisture is trapped below. Don't forget that the same rule applies to your body after a bath or shower.

• Which one? Do use creams over lotions. The American Academy of Dermatology says that creams are more effective for dry skin than lotions.

• Did you know that a dull blade can dry skin? Change your razor blade after every five to seven shaves. Think about your husband too!

• Warm water is always better than hot. Including a capful of emulsifying oil in your bath will also help maintain the dewy-soft skin we all crave.

• When we feel dryness, often what we are feeling is a thick layer of dead cells. This is self perpetuating because dry skin encourages dead-cell buildup. Exfoliation or skin smoothing is key to maintaining a hydrated, healthy, and vibrant look to your skin.

• What about water? While important for your overall health, unfortunately our skin is not like a plant and it doesn't directly absorb the water we drink. Instead, water undergoes a lengthy internal process before it ever reaches our skin cells.

• Exercise is hugely important as it helps bring nutrients and hydration to our skin cells.

BREAKING THE CODE

5 TOP REASONS YOUR SKIN AGES HOW TO STOP AND REPAIR THE DAMAGE

04

REASON #1
FREE-RADICAL DAMAGE

One of the hottest topics in the medical literature today is oxidative damage. Not only has oxidative damage been found to be a key factor in the development of disease, it is also one of the major factors causing skin aging.

EXTERNAL THREAT

We've all heard about the many different toxins that inhabit our environment—such things as cigarette smoke, air pollution, ozone, volatile organic chemicals, and much, much more. But while you are no doubt aware that this chemical soup is bad for your health, were you also aware that all these environmental toxins are especially bad for your skin?

They are.

These environmental toxins prevent your skin from remaining young—it's that simple—and they do it in a particularly damaging way. Cells break down under the assault of these chemicals, and their protective barriers leak. This breach of the cell wall enables even more toxins to enter, doing further damage and creating highly damaging atoms, or

groups of atoms, known as free radicals. Free radicals are created when certain environmental toxins react with oxygen.

A WORST-CASE SCENARIO

In the worst-case scenario, the invasion of toxins and its accompanying flood of free radicals makes its way to your skin's DNA. Free radicals are a huge threat to your skin's DNA, and its youthfulness, because it causes your skin to repair itself in all sorts of unnatural, malformed ways. The result? Anything from wrinkles to age spots to cancer. Because of the widespread damage they cause to the human body, scientists often call free radicals "indiscriminate drive-by shooters." The older you get the more important these players are for your skin, and for its overall health and beauty.

But don't be lulled into a false sense of security just because you manage to minimize the amount of environmental toxins to which you are exposed. Anytime you leave your home or office, your skin is in direct contact with the #1 free-radical generator: the sun.

INTERNAL THREAT

Of course, the outside of your body isn't the only part exposed to toxins each and every day. So is the inside. Stress, poor nutrition, preservatives, pesticides—they all are internal threats to your youthful skin, and they all add up. Did you know that just a single puff of cigarette smoke generates a free-radical "hit" to every cell of your body, accelerating the aging process? It's true, and the effect is very real, and very damaging.

EXACTLY WHAT ARE FREE RADICALS?

So we've explored the effect that free radicals have on your skin, but what exactly are they? And, since we're asking that question, let's ask a couple more while we're at it. Why weren't free radicals much of a threat to us when we were younger, and why should we be more concerned about them as we age?

Free radicals are atoms missing an electron. This makes them very hungry for another electron, and they will steal one wherever they can. The result is that they quite literally chip away at your skin cells. Molecule by molecule, they can break down the barrier membrane of your skin cells, which is the pathway they take all the way to your DNA.

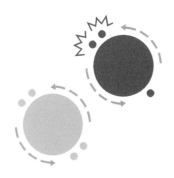

Free radicals are made of atoms missing an electron. They become unstable or "radical."

A free radical steals an electron from a healthy atom located on a cell membrane, helping create an entry way for other free radicals to enter the cell.

Antioxidants have electrons that they donate to a free radical. The cell membrane is spared because the free radical is kept "happy" by the donation of an electron from an antioxidant.

THE PERFECT WORLD
OF OUR YOUTH

In our youth, when we enjoyed smooth, beautiful skin, we were assaulted by free radicals each and every day—the same as we are today. The difference between then and now, however, is that when we were younger our skin had its own built-in defense system of antioxidants to fight off the free radical drive-bys. Our cells were in a perfect world—a youthful world where our cells had everything they needed to renew and repair themselves perfectly!

As we know, that perfect world scenario fades away as we age. By about age 30, the skin's own built-in antioxidant defense system begins to decline—so much so that by the age of 60, it is just a shadow of what it was at age 30.

So, just how important are antioxidants to maintaining healthy, youthful skin? Scientists have discovered that nature intended for you to have extremely high levels of antioxidants in your skin. In fact, when levels of these naturally protective agents were measured throughout the body, researchers found that the highest levels were distributed closest to the surface of the skin. What happens as we age is that these high levels decreases dramatically. Unfortunately, our skin produces lower levels of antioxidants at the exact time that we are entering a phase of life when our skin is in a perpetual state of oxidative stress. This oxidative stress occurs when more free radicals exist than can be neutralized by the quantity of antioxidants in our bodies. A stressed-out lifestyle, fast food on the run, poor sleeping habits, no sunscreen, and more all lead to a lifestyle where your skin cells can become permanently damaged in this maladaptive world.

age Breakers

THE CHOICE IS YOURS

We all hear about the latest discoveries of some powerful new antioxidants. But while these new discoveries are exciting, it's important to keep in mind that even the strongest antioxidant in the world won't be entirely effective if it leaves some part of the cell unprotected. It's just that simple. If cellular spaces are left unguarded, then havoc may occur. And believe me, you don't want that to happen within your skin. So the combination of free-radical fighters you choose is extremely important.

CHOOSE A VARIETY OF ANTIOXIDANTS

Free radicals create their own pathways of destruction. They start at the cell membrane and work their way deep into the cell's interior. It may not seem like much, but in the world of molecular biology, the cell is a HUGE area to protect. Different antioxidants protect different areas of our cells. Scientists have learned, for example, that some antioxidants protect around the fatty membrane or exterior of the cell, while others protect the watery interior of the cell. Researchers recommend choosing from both classes—the water soluble and the fat soluble—in order to ensure full protection.

Many people get lulled into a false sense of security by picking a lotion or serum with only one powerful antioxidant—say, grape seed extract or resveratrol (fat soluble), for example. If you are using only one antioxidant for protection of your skin, just be sure you supplement that antioxidant with another from the opposite class. If you do decide to use only one antioxidant, then lipoic acid is a good choice. It is not only a network antioxidant, but it is one of the very few antioxidants that is both fat and water soluble, meaning that it can do its magic in every part of the cell.

A POWERFUL COMBINATION

When you aim for my recommendation of including vitamins C and E in your regimen, you are not only choosing powerful network antioxidants (pg. 88), you are also including one from each class. This ensures full protection. No wonder we see so many proven skin benefits with this proven combination, from collagen building to UV protection—the list goes on and on. Learn more about skincare antioxidants from magazine ads and cosmetic counters in your Skin Pearls Glossary. You'll learn which class they fall into as well as the strengths to look for—and the weaknesses to be aware of.

How does your choice add up? Have you included combinations that shield the entire skin cell? If not, then you should. A small addition or change in your antioxidant regimen can spell significant—and youthful—benefits for years to come.

FREE RADICAL DAMAGE

Age Breakers

GO FOR THE GOLD

When deciding which topical antioxidants to use, I recommend starting with the gold standard: vitamin C (ascorbic acid). It has deservedly earned its title because in so many proven ways it goes above and beyond just quenching free radicals. One of the added benefits is that it has been documented to stimulate collagen synthesis. In fact, vitamin C is essential for each and every step of the process.

As you may know, our bodies don't manufacture vitamin C, so you need to ingest it through your diet or supplements. But in addition to increasing vitamin C levels in your blood, topical use of vitamin C is also necessary for achieving not only the youth-building collagen synthesis, but also for many other benefits as well. These benefits include:

1. Protection from harmful effects of the sun.

2. Improvement in skin luminosity through suppression of melanin formation.

3. Increase in the number of fibroblasts—the cells in your body that produce collagen.

4. DNA repair in those all-important fibroblast cells.

While there is a wealth of data confirming the antioxidant benefits of vitamin C, there are a couple of hitches. As an antioxidant, it is very unstable and may be slightly irritating to some. To address these issues, scientists have recently developed several derivatives to make vitamin C more stable and user friendly.

What do the similarities and differences mean to you? Read about what strengths to look for and what to expect in the Skin Pearls Glossary.

Age Breakers

THE POWER OF THE NETWORK

What if some antioxidants had special powers that set them apart from other antioxidants? Well—guess what? Some do.

Until recently, it was believed that antioxidants worked independently from one another. It was also believed that after a friendly antioxidant "donates" an electron to neutralize a free radical, the friendly antioxidant becomes weakened and may even develop into a free radical itself. Scientists have recently discovered, however, that certain antioxidants prevent this process from occurring. In a nutshell, they fuel one another and greatly extend their potency and lifespan.

For example, if vitamin E is added to vitamin C, the potency for preventing UV-generated free radicals in the skin goes up four fold. And if ferulic acid is added into the mix, the overall potency goes up a whopping eight fold. Look for combinations of these three nutrients to pay big dividends for skin shielding.

1 + 1 + 1 really can add up to 8!

Other powerful network antioxidants to look for are lipoic acid, CoQ10 (coenzyme Q10), and glutathione.

CEF

ASK THE
EXPERT

Dr. Barbara Schell

Dermatologist and Cosmetic Surgeon

Dr. Barbara Schell is a much sought-after dermatologist and cosmetic surgeon in Seattle, Washington. She received her medical degree from Indiana School of Medicine and has been in practice for 27 years. She is a member of the American Academy of Cosmetic Surgery as well as the American Academy of Dermatology. Her practice—Ageless Center for Rejuvenation—has received high accolades due to her pioneering spirit and expertise embracing newer, more-effective, and longer-lasting procedures and treatments. Her patients call her a perfectionist, and the press—such as InStyle magazine—rely on her advice and wisdom.

It is with great pleasure that Dr. Schell has agreed to share some of her wisdom regarding skincare with us today.

Q: Dr. Schell, first I want to just say that your skin looks absolutely flawless! You are a recognized physician for your expertise in the field of anti-aging dermatology as well as cosmetic surgery! Today we're hoping that you could share with my readers some take-home points about antioxidants and anti-aging skincare.

A: Antioxidants are an important part of the mix when it comes to anti-aging. Efficacy from these antioxidants will depend upon the amount of antioxidants in a formulation, its availability to the cells, the actual type of antioxidant, and the other properties of the formulation. But more on that later. First let's talk skincare in general. One of the things I want your readers to know is that even if they've been less

than stellar, even if they have sun damage, have been a smoker, or had a lot of stress in their lives and have not taken care of themselves, they can reverse the signs of aging. Anti-aging topicals do work to repair, protect, and rebuild. Besides antioxidants, which protect skin, other agents that work well are those that build collagen, such as peptides and growth factors.

Q: Is there one antioxidant that's "ahead of the pack" so to speak?

A: Probably the topical antioxidants most researched are the tretinoins and vitamin C. Vitamin C is an important co-factor for collagen production and has many other anti-aging qualities as well. But readers need to be mindful that percentages of vitamin C or other antioxidants in a skincare preparation really do matter, as well as the formulation content they are packaged in. There are many new and emerging antioxidants that may prove to be more important and effective.

Q: Okay. Let's talk skincare in general and ask the question everyone wants to know about: What makes a skincare line effective? Are there any basic rules we should be aware of?

A: Well, that's a definite yes. I educate my patients and viewers on my YouTube site "DoctorAgeless" about just that—what makes a skincare line effective or not. I would like to start with one bit of key information. It is a huge secret that the cosmetic industry does not want the public to know about. It will help your readers make better decisions on how to spend their money and get fabulous anti-aging results for their skin.

Q: Please elaborate!

A: First, your readers need to know that the price of a product does not equate with efficacy. In other words, just because you spend a lot more money on your skincare, it does not mean it's any better! It may feel better, it may sound better, the advertising may be fancier, but it doesn't mean it's going to work. So, here are the facts. By definition, if a skincare product actually makes a real, quantifiable change in your skin, or in other words, if it makes any kind of significant reversal of aging, it has to by law be sold as a prescription product, or in a doctor's office under their direction. I don't care how much you spend on your skincare—even if you spend $1,200. By law, an active that makes a statistically significant change in your skin cells requires it to be dispensed as prescription product.

So if you are being marketed to, being advertised to—which you are a million times a day—that this product is going to make a visible change in your skin within the next 24 hours, then it is just a temporary effect that has no long-term reversal of aging or collagen building. The body simply does not work this way. Products that build collagen or truly reverse the signs of aging require time.

Q: But what about women who swear that a department store skincare line works well for them?

A: Let's talk a little about what's really happening to your readers' skin when they are using most store-bought brands. For decades and decades, most cosmetic manufacturer skincare formulations were based on one premise only. That premise is all about plumping up the dead skin cell layer on the skin called the stratum corneum. The stratum corne-um is similar to a layer of a basket weave. It consists of dead skin cells that have not been shed off and it acts like a sponge, actually a very dry sponge. You can imagine that if you put water on a dry sponge, it's going to expand and become plump. That's exactly how almost all department store or drug-store skincare products work. They go into the dead skin cell layer, bind to it and plump it up with fluid, usually water or perhaps even hylauronic acid and temporarily expand that layer of dry skin cells. As a result, it's going to make your dead skin cells—your stratum corneum—look better. It may feel absolute-ly luscious, but it's a very temporary effect. That's how the big manufacturers claim that you're going to see a visible difference in the next 24 to 48 hours. The problem is 4 or 5 hours later, 10 hours later, the next morning, you're going to wake up and look exactly the same as you did before you used the product. And that's okay if that's what you're looking for. I simply want your readers to know what's really happening. You're not going to get any true reversal of the aging process that's going to have any lasting benefit. It's simply a temporary plumping of your dead skin, making it look good for a short period of time. What's more, when it wears off, you're right back to square one.

Q: What about products that claim to have active known anti-aging ingredients in them such as vita-min C or glycolic acid?

A: There is another important distinction between store-bought and physician-based skincare. The other thing readers need to know is that if a product says that they have an active ingredient in them such a glycolic acid, more often than not they do not contain enough of that ingredient to make a signifi-cant difference in your skin

Q: Please tell us more!

A: Let's take a perfect example. Let's say that we're talking about glycolic acid. We know that from all the studies over many years that glycolic acid does in fact stimulate new collagen production. It does thicken your epidermis and your dermis, so it is anti-aging and it will reduce some signs of your lines and wrinkles. However what the cosmetic companies don't tell you is that they don't use the amounts of glycolic acid proven to generate collagen production. In studies quantifying collagen-building benefits, at least a 15% concentration of glycolic acid is included in the formulation.

When it comes to glycolic acid, not only is the percentage important, but the pH as well. If the pH is too high or if the pH is too low, the product may be neutralized or simply not work at all. Manufacturers more often than not include a very small percentage such as 1% or 2% in their formulations. Rarely, they increase the levels up to 8% (which is very high for an over-the-counter skincare product). Simply put and scientifically confirmed, 8% is not going to give you a real change like 15% is. Is it better than nothing? Yes, of course it is, but it's not going to give you the same changes you're hoping for. The marketing is deceptive because the percentages that bring about real changes are not used. And quite

frankly, most of these companies put a very small percentage in their products just so they can say that it's in their product. For example, they may even put 0.01% of an active ingredient in there just to say that it's in there.

So once again, just remember that most of the drugstore and department store products work on a temporary basis and plump up the skin, and/or the amounts they may have of an active ingredient is too low to be active.

Q: That is an important difference! Dr. Schell, because we're talking skincare let's turn to the topic of toners. Why are women still using them? What's the real story about them?

A: Toners have been around a really long time, and there's always this controversy: do I need a toner or do I not need a toner? Here are the facts. Toners were originally created because most of the soaps we used back in the good old days had a very, very high pH. They stripped the skin of all its oils and left the skin dry and usually with some sort of coating on it from lye, calcium, magnesium, or other things that were in the soaps. They left the skin pH at about a 9 or a 10. That is not a healthy pH for the skin. This explains the reasons toners were invented. It was to bring the pH of the skin back down to the normal healthy level of about 4.5 or 5. You don't need a toner unless you're using a harsh, soap-based product, which we do not encourage that you do. We encourage that you use an appropriate cleanser that has the proper balance to be in homeostasis with your skin. So honestly, there's no need for you to spend your money on a toner.

Q: Dr. Schell, this information is invaluable to my readers. Now I have to ask you, do you have a favorite skincare line?

A: The answer would have to be Skin Medica. Skin Medica is a world-class company that specializes in the arena of growth factors and skin anti-aging. The cornerstone product is the TNS Essential Serum. The product is unique because it contains 110 different growth factors and cytokines. This is incredibly state of the art, patented, and one of the best products on the market today. Growth factors are a huge advancement in anti-aging skincare, and Skin Medica is on the forefront of this research and development.

Thank you Dr. Schell. My readers and I thank you for enlightening us about real world skin care!

SUN

04

REASON #2 • SUN

Deep, course wrinkles, patchy discoloration, age spots, dilated blood vessels , elastosis, and dryness are sure signs of prolonged sun exposure. The high-energy UV rays, traveling at the remarkably fast speed of 186,000 miles per second from the sun's surface to well below the outer layer of your skin, have consequences that until recently has not been fully understood by the medical community as well as the general public.

Accounting for roughly 90% of extrinsic aging, UV rays generated by the sun (and by tanning beds and other devices) are without a doubt the most powerful and pervasive reason our skin ages. Powerful because even a brief exposure sets off a destructively aging mechanism that can last hours if not days after the initial encounter. Pervasive because the ozone layer is shrinking and our exposure to UV radiation is increasing.

SECONDS COUNT

When we think about sun damage, we usually think of a "long-term" effect, but new research has proven otherwise. While long-term effects of the sun such as skin cancers and age spots are well-documented, new research now explains how wrinkles, loose skin, and creases are created in the short term. A few minutes of sun exposure by an unprotected face, arm, or leg literally turns on a switch deep within your skin to break down its protein matrix, ultimately leading to the development of wrinkles. Even if you

don't get a sunburn or a tan there are a whole plethora of changes occurring deep inside your skin that even the richest, most-expensive moisturizer can't stop. In a nutshell, short-term exposure — as short as 15 minutes—has a whole new meaning. What do these short-term effects mean to you? Read on.

UV exposure generates extremely high levels of free radicals triggering tiny "hits" to cells deep within your skin. That in turn stimulates an inflammatory response and the whole inflammatory/free radical cascade begins. These factors will ultimately lead to detrimental long-term consequences such as age spots, discoloration, and sadly even to skin cancer. But what are the powerful short-term effects? Scientists have discovered that it takes the sun just minutes to trigger a skin-degrading enzyme to increase many thousand fold. This enzyme is now believed to play the number-one major role in the development of wrinkles and slack skin. This class of enzymes, called metalloproteinases, is popping up more and more in the research into the how's and whys of aging skin. MMP's are found in abundance under each and every wrinkle you see.

Why do you need to know about them? Consider this: the firmness, smoothness, elasticity—in short, your skin's youthfulness—depends on the levels of your skins MMPs being in balance. MMPs are enzymes, and as we all know, enzymes break down and demolish things. Think of them as demolition

crews that play a role in healthy skin to clear away matter so that wound healing can occur. Aging, particularly wrinkles, occurs when for no apparent reason your levels of MMPs rise. UV rays are one of the biggest triggers for these MMPs to turn into massive wrecking crews breaking apart your dermal matrix. Other triggers are pollutants, chlorinated water, smoking, and even normal aging. In general, anything that increases skin irritation, inflammation, and the production of free radicals can increase your levels of MMPs. Yet sun exposure is the worst. Sadly, new research has documented that a brief sun exposure can increase MMP levels several thousand fold. These abnormally high levels of MMPs can remain activated in the skin for up to a week.

The good news is that recent research into the effects of UV exposure has led to the development of powerful actives that have the potential to help repair, control, and prevent the damage. Scientists have discovered that even the most-potent SPF product will not completely block the rise of free radicals that increase the enzyme levels. Potent antioxidants have been shown to quell free radicals and consequently MMP generation. In addition, novel actives called MMP inhibitors have a direct blocking effect on the enzymes themselves. Very few agents can actually reverse sun damage, but there is a proven winner in the war against wrinkles.

A PROVEN TOPICAL THAT REVERSES SUN DAMAGE

Chemicals related to vitamin A callled retinoids (tretinoin, tazarotene). These products help repair skin damage due to sunburn and natural aging, such as fine wrinkles, liver spots, and rough skin. It may take months before the skin shows improvement. Side effects include redness, scaling, burning, and itching, which can be treated with corticosteroid cream. Sunscreen needs to be applied during the day because vitamin A products can cause the skin to be sensitive to sunlight. Warning: Women who are pregnant or think they are pregnant should not use any product related to vitamin A. Oral tretinoin is known to cause birth defects. Topical tretinoin may also cause birth defects.

"Despite the baggage, Retin - A is proven winner in the war against sun damage. However, if the side effects concern you, read on about newer alternatives such as retinaldehyde – similar efficacy, but with much fewer side effects. See page 220."

THINGS YOU SHOULD KNOW ABOUT

Everyone needs sun protection. Due to an increased amount of melanin, many people of color enjoy a greater amount of sun protection. Their skin ages at a slower rate than white skin. However, it doesn't mean they should ignore using a good sunscreen. For example, in a 2010 study, black women living in Florida had a 60% higher rate of melanoma than black women living elsewhere. Everyone, no matter what race, needs full sun protection.

UVA rays stream right through glass. They penetrate the deepest and create the most damage. Besides wrinkles, they are particularly responsible for age spots often found on the hands and face. What's more, unlike UVB rays they are pretty consistent throughout the day and throughout the year. Unless you dwell 24/7 in a basement, daily sunscreen should be the foundation of your beauty regimen.

Broader is much better. It's critical that you choose a sunscreen that protects against both UVA and UVB rays. When you read an SPF label, the number refers only to protection against UVB rays. That's because shortwave UVB rays cause sunburn. Remember that UVA rays are more damaging and more aging. They penetrate deep down in the dermis, altering DNA and triggering collagen

demolition enzymes to go haywire. Look for labels with the wording "Broad Spectrum." The ingredients avobenzone, zinc oxide, and ecamsule give the most-complete UVA protection.

TANNING BEDS

If catching indoor rays is part of your beauty routine – think again. Tanning beds use fluorescent bulbs that emit mostly UVA, with smaller doses of UVB. The UVA radiation used in the beds is up to three times more intense than the UVA in natural sunlight. A quick tan, right? Remember that UVA rays penetrate more deeply and are the main cause of photo aging. Even more, a recent Mayo Clinic study reported an astonishing 705% increase in the incidence of developing one of the deadliest forms of skin cancer, melanoma. This increase is occurring among Caucasian women, ages 18 to 25, and is thought to be linked to the high use of indoor tanning beds among that population. Yikes!

15 MINUTES OF SUN

THE COUNTDOWN BEGINS...

UVB UVA

Once believed to have only a minor effect on skin, UVA rays are now believed to be the major contributor to photo aging. With it's longer wavelengths, UVA rays penetrate more deeply in skin, work more efficiently, and are much more abundant (95%UVA and 5%UVB).

FREE RADICALS

Sunlight is the number-one causal factor for free radical generation in skin. A brief exposure creates high levels that start a chain reaction under the skin's surface. What follows is a cascading process of destruction.

ENZYMES

MMPs, the enzymes responsible for chopping away at the dermal matrix, become abnormally elevated. These unnaturally high levels remain elevated (roughly 1,000 fold) for at least one week after a 15-minute unprotected sun exposure.

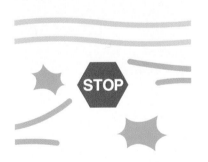

COLLAGEN

Skin stops manufacturing what it needs most to remain youthful —its collagen network—for an entire 24 to 48 hour period. UV penetration decreases skin's ability to express an important growth factor needed for collagen generation to occur..

INFLAMMATION

Inflammation is triggered as skin tries to repair itself. There becomes an influx of damaging inflammatory mediators that trigger more cascading events.

SOLAR SCAR

A brief exposure creates a tiny "solar scar" unseen by the naked eye. But after 100, 200, 500 exposures, these invisible scars coalesce into a scar you can see. You see it as wrinkles or sagging skin that makes you look old well before your time.

Age Breakers

A REVERSAL OF TIME

MIRACLES CAN HAPPEN

We've learned a bit about our skin cells. One of the things we've learned is that the outside of our skin cells are equipped with receptors that act like tiny locks. (See illustration.) Magic happens when a key comes along that happens to fit elegantly into one of these locks. Remember the powerful lock-and-key mechanism hormones use to control our skin cells ? By understanding the powerful force of cell communication through receptors, scientists have developed a substance that can talk directly to the skin cell—reversing not all, but much of the sun damage you thought was there for good.

Believe it or not, our skin cells are born with tiny retinic acid or Retin-A-specific receptors. When switched on by their lock-and-key biologic mechanism, these receptors create all kinds of miracles, one of many being the repair of sun damage. This powerful mechanism works in the following ways—and more:

• The powerful enzymes that try to break apart much of your dermis are greatly reduced.

• Your skin cells are replaced more rapidly, creating a vibrant appearance.

• Circulation to your skin cells increases as the tiny capillaries responsible for feeding your skin multiply in both reach and number.

• Your collagen levels (safety net) get a tremendous bump up, resulting in a major impact on wrinkle reduction.

• That mottled, sun-damaged appearance begins to fade completely over time.

• Pore size is reduced. Yeah! Most of us would welcome that.

Retin-A is so effective that the FDA gave it a seal of approval as the only topical agent proven to repair aging and sun-damaged skin. That seal of approval takes an overwhelming amount of highly controlled studies.

So, what's the catch? Well, first of all, because Retin-A was originally used to treat acne, it was never viewed by the general public to be an anti-aging agent. It's also hugely irritating to most everyone's skin. One of the big reasons it's viewed as too intolerable to use is that most of us were never shown how to use it properly, and so we gave up on it altogether.

In an effort to address the irritation problem of Re-tin-A, we have officially entered the age of retinols. Retinols are the skincare industry's answer to Ret-in-A's irritation problem. We've been told by many retinol manufacturers they are one and the same, but they're really not. The problem is that your skin cells do not contain retinol receptors. Not a single one. Your skin cells do of course contain retinic acid receptors, which is why Retin-A works. If the retinol you applied to your skin managed to reach the cell wall, it would be turned away. It's that simple. How-ever, the skin can do something magical. It can con-vert the retinol you applied to your skin into Retin-A, and once it does, then it can in turn work its magic on the skin cells. But wait—there's a catch. Not all of us can convert enough of the ineffective retinol into the effective Retin-A. Certain retinols are more easily converted by our skin, so if we decide to use products containing retinols, we'll want to focus on the ones that are most effective. Read about them in the Skin Pearls Glossary. I provide you with tips in making either approach, whether it's the Retin-A or the more natural retinol route, effective and tolerable for your sun-damaged skin.

Your skin cells have a multitude of tiny receptors. Hormones, vitamin D, and prescription retinol all have unique keys that can unlock a specific receptor site on each skin cell. Once the key and lock fit together, mira-cles can happen. In the case of Retin-A or prescription retinol, your skin cells are stimulated to reverse sun damage

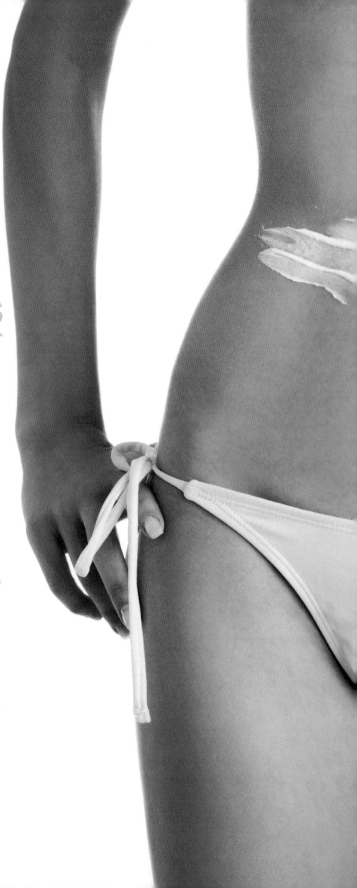

Age Breakers

HALF MEASURES

Scientists have discovered that most of the free radicals generated in our skin by UV light are not prevented by even the broadest spectrum of sunscreen. Even when they are applied perfectly (as few of us actually do), sunscreens have been found to put a halt to only about 55 percent of free-radical generation. Remember, those free radicals or indiscriminate shooters are triggering all kinds of aging events in your skin. They start a cascade effect of inflammatory cells—making the deleterious enzymes in your body go into overdrive. while eating away at your skin cells like sparks from a fireplace eating away at a nearby carpet. Antioxidants have the power to neutralize these marauders, and they should be a key part of your regimen.

MOP UP THE WHOLE MESS, NOT HALF

Consider applying an antioxidant in conjunction with your sunscreen. Committing your skin to 100 percent protection instead of just 50 percent will pay huge dividends over the course of your life. Believe me, you'll thank yourself many times over.

Age Breakers

A SMARTER SUNSCREEN

Along with activating the MMPs (matrix metallopro-teinases), which are enzymes that literally eat your inner skin apart, the sun can cause serious damage to your skin's DNA. Tiny imperfections accumulate over time and have tremendous consequences. These seemingly simple flaws result in everything from wrinkles, hyperpigmentation, and loss of texture and tone, to serious skin cancers.

What if there were more-advanced sunscreens that not only protected skin from UV rays, but that could reach our skin's fragile DNA strands, protect them, and help repair the damage created by years under the sun?

It's hard to believe, but it's true. The new era of smart sunscreens has arrived! Scientists have invented powerful enzymes that are able to recog-nize and cut out damaged DNA in the skin, which in turn triggers the skin's DNA to regenerate. These enzymes are so effective that they have even been proven to reverse pre-cancerous growths in patients with severely sun-damaged skin.

When we were younger, our cells had a toolbox full of these DNA-repairing enzymes. But as we age, our repair enzymes go into a decline mode, and the damage to our skin steadily accumilates.

HOW DOES IT WORK?

UV light damages skin by causing chemical bonds to form in the wrong places along the DNA molecules in skin cells. Topically applied, highly efficient enzymes—often harvested from marine organisms—work by cutting out the damaged bits of DNA which are then regenerated. Researchers have found these enzymes to be effective and look to this path of research for potential answers in the war against UV-induced skin cancer.

Age Breakers

REALITY CHECK

As you've read through this chapter, you've probably been thinking to yourself, "Yikes—I had no idea how damaging the sun can be!" It really is alarming to think of what's going on in our skin as we encounter the sun—for even as little as 15 minutes. But a lot of us mistakenly believe that we don't need to be concerned if we're not outdoors for any significant amount of time during the course of the day. I've fallen victim to this way of thinking myself. While being religious about applying sunscreen and topical antioxidants for my face and neck each and every day, no matter rain or shine, I always neglected my hands because quite frankly it seemed like too much trouble for my busy schedule. And after all I'm just running back and forth between my car and medical clinics, right? Well, reality caught up with me when I was least expecting it. While I'm pleased with the appearance of my facial skin, I'm a bit saddened each time I glance down at my 60-year-old hands. I don't feel that old, and my face still has a youthful appearance. Why should my hands have to reflect my age? It's because I never gave them the reality check that they deserved.

Don't forget yours!

"It's more difficult to repair sun damage on body parts other than your face. Don't forget your ankles, arms and calves!"

Dr. Misbah Khan

Founder and President of MKhan Dermatology

Dr. Misbah Khan, Founder and President of MKhan Dermatology and Clinical Assistant Professor of Dermatology at Weill Cornell Medical College at New York Presbyterian Hospital, is nationally and internationally recognized for her innovative contributions toward the therapeutic applications of lasers in dermatology, fat grafting for facial asymmetries and deformities, treatment of cellulite, and for total body contouring and cutaneous oncology. Dr. Khan also works directly with the leading laser companies in pioneering the latest technologies regarding treatment of cellulite, skin rejuvenation, and laser-assisted tattoo removal.

Q: Dr. Kahn, according to the American Cancer Society, skin cancer is on the rise and accounts for about half of all cancers in the United States each year. As a skin cancer surgeon and specialist, would you mind dispelling some of the myths surrounding this critical topic?

A: I would be happy to! There are many misconceptions regarding protection. Lets discuss some of the more popular myths.

Myth #1: People with darker skin who rarely burn are more immune to skin cancer development.

Truth: Protection from the sun is imperative no matter what skin type you happen to be. This is because the three most common skin cancers—squamous cell, basal cell, and melanoma—are related to cumulative sun exposure. Everyone, regardless of skin color, needs to use sunscreen with a high enough SPF, or better yet, fully protect themselves from UV rays. Skin cancers are commonly seen in patients with naturally dark skin as well as pale skin. Keep in mind that even if you always tan and don't burn, skin cancer is still a possibility.

Myth #2: As long as I check myself for unusual spots, I don't need to undergo skin cancer screening.

Truth: Everyone should have their skin checked once a year by a board-certified dermatologist in addition to self-screening for unusual growths. If cancers such as melanoma go unchecked, they can spread throughout the body, rendering deadly consequences. It is critical that you do your homework and find a dermatologist who has the training and background in the arena of skin cancer. For detailed information about skin cancer and skin protection, I recommend you visit www.aad.org or www.skincancer.org.

Myth #3: When I use a foundation or moisturizer with a built-in SPF, I'm protected for the entire day.

Truth: These are good products to use only if your sun exposure is limited. If any outdoor activity is planned, these products will only suffice if ample amounts are applied—a marble's size for the face and at least a golf ball amount for the body. Also, please keep in mind that these products need to be applied every two hours if any outdoor activities are involved. As a general rule, most people don't apply enough sunscreen to render themselves protected to the numerical amount printed on the bottle.

Myth #4: It's better for me to get vitamin D naturally through sun exposure.

Truth: While it's true that many people are vitamin D deficient, exposing one's skin to the sun unprotected is not the answer. Even if you exposed your entire nude body for a full 20 minutes of unprotected UV rays, your body would only produce one-quarter to one-third of the required amount of vitamin D for the day. Vitamin D supplements are safe and cost pennies, but more important, do not cause skin cancer nor premature aging. Vitamin D fortified foods—milk, yogurt, cereals, fatty fish—are also recommended.

Q: Dr. Khan, how does skin cancer manifest itself, and what happens if skin cancer goes undetected?

A: Skin cancer melanoma is the uncontrolled growth of abnormal color-producing cells or melanocytes in the different layers of the skin. Screening is vital because if left unchecked, these cancers can spread from the skin into other tissues and organs. Basal cell carcinoma is the most common skin cancer in the world. Your readers should be aware that skin cancers may have many different appearances. They can be small, shiny, waxy, scaly and rough, firm and red, crusty or bleeding, or have other characteristics. Again, it is imperative that any suspicious growth or spot be examined by a board-certified dermatologist.

Q: Dr. Khan, let's turn the focus back to skin aging. There is a lot of buzz these days about the newer, non-invasive treatments that can take years off a person's appearance, but people are a little confused because progress in lasers and fillers is rapid and it is difficult for the average person to stay

current, let alone to understand. Your input would be invaluable to my readers because you are a nationally and internationally recognized expert in the development of these newer treatments.

In your practice, you harness the latest technologies and offer your patients an investment in themselves. You termed it your BFF™ method. Your BFF™ strategy is unique because it encompasses most, if not all, aspects of facial aging without surgery. Please let my readers know more about your synergistic BFF™ method.

Let's start with the letter B. What does it stand for, and what type of facial aging does it correct?

A: B stands for Botulinum toxin, more commonly known as Botox®. Botox® treats a type of wrinkle or fold created by repeated movement. For example, when you squint, the muscles around your eyes contract and cause crow's feet. When you frown, the muscles between your brows contract, causing your skin to furrow. Because facial muscles are attached to outlying skin, contraction of these muscles causes the skin to bunch together, forming creases, folds, or lines between the bulk of the muscle. These wrinkles are mild when we are young, but become deeper and more noticeable as we age.

Botox® is administered in the form of an intramuscular injection that specifically affects the muscle movements beneath the skin to relax the underlying muscle activity that causes these types of wrinkles to form over time. It stops the release of a chemical neurotransmitter, acetylcholine, responsible for muscle contraction. In other words, it prevents signals from the nerve cells to reach the muscles, effectively leaving the muscles without instructions to contract. Results can be seen in as little as 24 to 48 hours.

Q: And F?

A: F stands for fractional lasers. I use many fractional lasers specifically tailored to my practice.

Q: How are fractional lasers an improvement over older lasers?

A: The Fraxel laser system is considered one of the best available treatments for non-ablative fractional resurfacing of the face, neck, chest, and hands. There are several different Fraxel platforms currently available to target different skin problems including, but not limited to, acne scars, fine lines, wrinkles, skin surface irregularities, skin pores, brown spots, and old scars. Fraxel resurfaces damaged skin to reveal younger, more refreshed skin, improving the overall appearance through a simple procedure with minimal downtime.

Q: How do they work?

A: The advanced Fraxel technology offers deeper dermal laser penetration—depths up to 1.6mm—than traditional treatments. Fraxel is a good nonsurgical alternative to rather aggressive laser resurfacing procedures as it significantly reduces the risks and recovery time associated with resurfacing procedures. Fraxel can also be considered a potentially preventative treatment, as it often eliminates the need for rather invasive surgical procedures.

Q: And, what are the results?

A: Results are outstanding and can take years, if not a decade, off a person's appearance. Most patients can achieve effective results after receiving three to five Fraxel treatment sessions spaced two to four weeks apart. Patients can return to work very quickly after each of these sessions, usually after 24 hours.

Q: It is truly wonderful to know that these lasers not only reverse signs of aging, but also prevent and even eliminate the need for surgical procedures in the future. During our initial discussion you spoke in depth about the final F: fillers. Can you share with our readers the role of fillers for rejuvenation?

A: First let me say that we often blame genetics and gravity for aging and sagging skin, but it's mainly the loss of volume underneath the skin which is responsible for earlier signs of aging. Today, most signs of aging can be reversed with simple procedures that are not only affordable, but give you the most natural, youthful appearance with little or no downtime.

I use hyaluronic acid-based fillers, as these are completely reversible, and the patient's own fat—harvested and then processed for injection in the office—in order to restore a youthful fullness to the face.

Q: Would you shed some light on the benefits of fat transfers?

A: Fat is a wonderful alternative to essentially any kind of filler that is used for face, breast, or buttock augmentation. Fat contains a wealth of stem cells and can be transferred from an area where a patient doesn't want it and be transferred to a new area. It makes an excellent, natural-looking filler, and along with the benefits of stem cells, the rejuvenating effects can be long term. The fat survival rate is 47% to 50% at 6 to 12 months. Because your own tissue is used, there is no chance for adverse or allergic reactions. Another benefit of fat transferring is that it can be cost effective when large volumes of filler are needed to restore facial fullness. Fat can be a cost-effective alternative to large volumes of fillers.

Q: Thanks Dr. Khan. Explaining how your BFF™ method synergistically corrects all aspects of facial aging can help us get up to speed on the latest laser and filler developments.

In our conversation, you cautioned against a trend that is rapidly occurring in the United States. Unfortunately, when someone is seeking laser rejuvenation, the entire process from diagnosis to the use of the laser itself is conducted by a staff person and not the doctor. What advice would you give my readers?

A: It's critical that you do your homework. Seek out a physician who is board certified in dermatologic surgery, head and neck plastic surgery, and oculoplastic surgery. At the very least, the doctor should conduct the diagnosis as well as the procedures, especially the lasers. Your face and your skin deserve the care of someone who has undergone years of specialized medical training.

Q: Great advice! Finally, I would be remiss if I didn't ask you about skincare. You mentioned that you think Retin-A is a powerful ally against UV damage and you also thought two skincare lines stood above the rest. What are they?

A: Definitely. There are two skincare lines that come to mind. Guerlain's®—their Orchidee Imperiale series is very good, especially for patients who have sensitive skin and are allergic to preservatives. Second is Dior® Diorsnow. Both are excellent choices.

INFLAMMATION

04

REASON #3 • INFLAMMATION

Often called the silent killer, chronic inflammation is a complex process that plays a major role in how fast we age. Experts now consider chronic inflammation to be the number-one common denominator for all major diseases. Its effects are so damaging that scientists have even developed a blood test to measure and determine if you are at higher risk of suffering its consequences, and today an increasing number of individuals are using this test to look at their chances of developing serious problems. This is how important a role inflammation plays in the aging process.

A SILENT KILLER

But how does chronic inflammation age the skin? In a nutshell, when you have inflammation in your skin, a shift in the skin's cellular process occurs, and your skin cells interact completely differently. This shift happens because your skin cells are always on the alert—looking for outsiders and foreign invaders, including bacteria and allergens. Inflammation starts when the body reads the skin as having a foreign invader that needs to be vanquished and rid of by being broken down and crushed. This unmerciful crushing of an enemy is a necessary step because

the invaders first need to be expelled before the healing process can begin. But what happens if this process of crush and kill never stops? What if it is an ongoing cycle with no end?

That's exactly what happens to your skin when you suffer from chronic inflammation. Your body produces an army of seek-and-destroy cells in your skin that operate 24 hours a day, 7 days a week—year after year—all the while destroying your skin's healthy tissue.

Think of it as a silent, slow, and drawn-out war that wreaks constant havoc on your skin.

When is inflammation a good thing? Acute inflammation is a normal healthy process your skin uses to rid itself of bacteria, allergens, and infections. Without it, infections would go unchecked and wounds would never heal. Inflammation rescues your skin by first recognizing the bacteria, killing, and engulfing it, thus breaking down the damaged tissue and sending it away so the skin is cleared for renewal to begin.

But when does a short healing crusade turn into a long, drawn-out war, and when does acute become chronic?

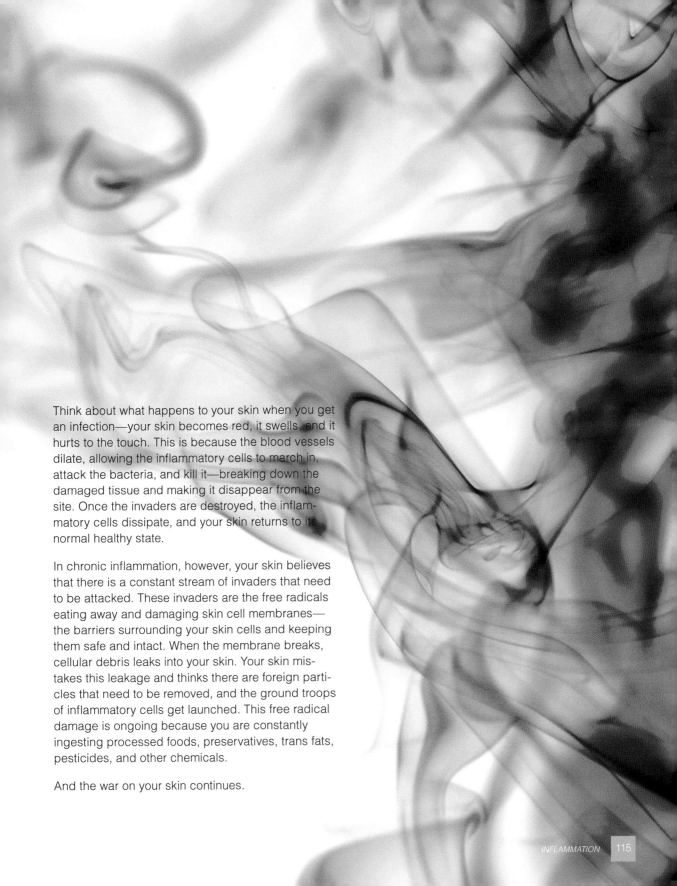

Think about what happens to your skin when you get an infection—your skin becomes red, it swells, and it hurts to the touch. This is because the blood vessels dilate, allowing the inflammatory cells to march in, attack the bacteria, and kill it—breaking down the damaged tissue and making it disappear from the site. Once the invaders are destroyed, the inflammatory cells dissipate, and your skin returns to its normal healthy state.

In chronic inflammation, however, your skin believes that there is a constant stream of invaders that need to be attacked. These invaders are the free radicals eating away and damaging skin cell membranes—the barriers surrounding your skin cells and keeping them safe and intact. When the membrane breaks, cellular debris leaks into your skin. Your skin mistakes this leakage and thinks there are foreign particles that need to be removed, and the ground troops of inflammatory cells get launched. This free radical damage is ongoing because you are constantly ingesting processed foods, preservatives, trans fats, pesticides, and other chemicals.

And the war on your skin continues.

The bottom line is that chronic and excessive inflammation is now considered to be the major culprit in visible signs of aging, and the destruction of normal tissue, especially elastin and collagen. Elastin and collagen play key roles in keeping your skin smooth and wrinkle free.

TRIGGERS

• PROCESSED FOODS
• HIGH GLYCEMIC INDEX FOODS
• HYDROGENATED FATS
• TRANS FATS

Facial products that irritate the skin, due to non-quality ingredients, inadequate moisturization of skin—it weakens the skin barrier. Stress revs up cortisol —a hormone that predisposes skin to inflammation.

• SKIPPING ON SLEEP
• CIGARETTE SMOKE
• AUTO EXHAUST
• POLLUTION
• EXPOSURE TO UV LIGHT
• STRESS
• SKIN IRRITANTS

DID YOU KNOW?

Stress causes the release of a destructive hormone called cortisol. Scientists sometimes refer to cortisol as the Dr. Jekyll and Mr. Hyde hormone because of the many serious health issues linked to it. In fact with our hectic lifestyles, it has become a public enemy number one

Scientists have known for years that elevated cortisol levels contributes to weight gain, loss of muscle mass, lower immune function, memory loss, and probably worst of all, lasting effects on our most precious commodity, our children. Researchers at Johns Hopkins report that when children are exposed to a chronically stressful environment, the elevated cortical levels change the expression of numerous genes linked to mental illness. They report that these developments predispose our kids to develop depression later on in their adult years.

"Watch out for stress. Besides skin aging, an increase in cortisol causes weight gain, a heightened risk of developing certain diseases and a whole host of other problems including long-term risk factors for our kids."

MENTAL DETOX

• Regular physical exercise Any regular aerobic activity, walking, jogging, swimming, biking has been documented to burn off excess cortisol levels.

• Loving-kindness meditation Meditation engages a nerve called the vagus nerve which triggers a signal to your nervous system to lower heart rate, blood pressure, and decrease cortisol.

• Connectivity Two studies published in the *Journal of Science* illustrate that isolation can lead to increased cortisol levels. Socialization is good for us.

CAN INFLAMMATION BE CONTROLLED?

Yes it can. There are many factors that determine how much inflammation you have in your body and skin. Food is one of them. Says Dr. Andrew Weil, "Without question diet influences inflammation."

It is now clear that destructive chronic inflammation can be prevented and reversed by consumption of proper foods and oral supplements, as well as by the application of topical actives.

Anti-inflammatory foods that optimize the skin's barrier function include...

FOODS RICH IN OMEGA-3 FATTY ACIDS

- Salmon
- Flaxseed
- Fish oil

AVOID THE FOLLOWING FOODS

- White flour
- Processed foods
- Sugar

TOPICAL ANTI-INFLAMMATORIES

- Vitamin C
- Green tea
- Licorice root
- Milk thistle
- Gotu kola

"Our skin reflects our diet almost immediately. If we consume fatty, sugary, and processed foods, our skin is likely to react by becoming inflamed, puffy, and rough in texture."

- Nicholas Perricone, M.D.

"Skin care regimens recommended by professionals for reversing and preventing visible skin aging should include products with active ingredients focused on reversing and preventing chronic inflammation. This change in strategy should occur with all topical products, oral supplements, and dietary recommendations."

- Carl Thornfeldt, M.D.

Age Breakers

BEAT INFLAMMATION UPSTREAM

Experts have discovered in recent years that free-radical or oxidative damage is one of the biggest culprits in the ramp up of inflammation in our skin cells. In fact, outside of autoimmune diseases such as rosacea, researchers now believe that free-radical damage to the skin cells is the starting point that triggers the long cascade of inflammatory events in the first place.

The good news is that free-radical damage to your skin is highly preventable. You can beat it, and your skin will look younger and more beautiful as a result.

Think of free radicals as the match that ignites a long, drawn-out forest fire. Trust me, a chronic state of inflammation is a tragic cascade of events that you don't want to endure. Your skin is unique from other organs in your body because it is under heavy assault from oxidative triggers each and every day. This is both bad news and good news. The bad news is that if you leave your skin unshielded from the free-radical assaults (and from sources of oxidative damage, including environmental toxins and the sun), you will most likely trigger the cascade that will lead to damaged skin. The good news is that you can put out

the fires by taking what physicians call "upstream action," using potent and proven antioxidants to nip the entire process in the bud.

Usually, the greater the antioxidant power, the greater the anti-inflammatory effects. One of the newest stars on the scene is alpha lipoic acid. This antioxidant—called "nature's powerhouse" by some—has a myriad of anti-aging qualities. Here are five in particular:

• Unlike many antioxidants, which aren't effective with all parts of the skin cell, alpha lipoic acid can work its miracles in both water and fat. This means that free radicals will be quenched in ALL parts of the cell.

• It inhibits damaging inflammatory cells directly, as well as quenching free radicals secreted by inflammatory cells.

• With normal aging, skin cells begin to function more slowly. Alpha lipoic acid increases the cells' energy levels by protecting the cells' energy source—the mitochondria. As a result, they start to behave more youthfully.

• It has been proven to trigger fibroblasts to produce more collagen, and may play a role in lessening glycation or sugar bonding.

• It is one of the "network antioxidants," meaning it fuels other antioxidants to work longer and harder—particularly glutathione, which is probably the body's most important antioxidant.

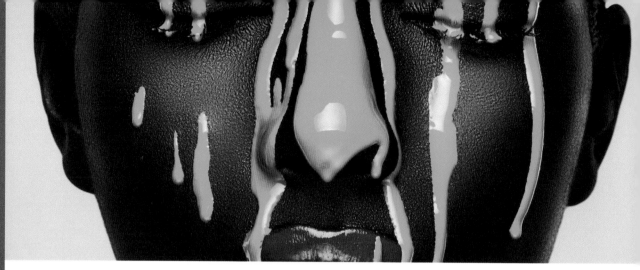

Age Breakers
A BALANCING ACT

Did you know that each day, deep inside our bodies, a balancing act is occurring? Our overall health, our ability to fight off many diseases, and even the aging process of our skin are all affected by our ability to get this balancing act right.

Scientists have discovered that as we age, our bodies may start a downhill slide into a cellular shift called chronic inflammation. This shifting process has been linked to many pro-inflammatory diseases, including cancer, heart disease, and autoimmune disorders. You may recall that chronic inflammation is a condition where the body mounts a slow army of defense against itself. So vital a topic is chronic inflammation that medical researchers have developed a blood test for one of its markers: a C-reactive protein (CRP) test. A high test result indicates the greater likelihood you may develop one of the inflammatory diseases.

So while chronic inflammation can now be tested for, until recently, no one had pinned down major causal factors leading to it. That situation has changed, and a major culprit has been identified. It is not found in any one food substance, but is instead the ratio of one food to another. To be exact, it is the ratio of omega-6 fatty acids (or even-numbered omegas)—the inflammation-pro-

ducing fats—to omega-3 fatty acids (or odd-numbered omegas), the inflammation quelling fats. Your body and your skin need both fats. They just need equal parts of each, in other words, a ratio of 1.

AN OIL SWITCH THAT INCLUDES A MULTITUDE OF BENEFITS

How does this balance of fats become critical to the health of our body and skin? Let's look back at our ancestors. Long, long ago, humans consumed on average the same percentage of omega-6 foods as omega-3s. That meant that their daily ratio was closer to that of a healthy number of 1. Over thousands and thousands of years of human development, this equal ratio may have even affected our how DNA evolved, meaning that we have become programmed to require this equal ratio of good-to-bad fats in our diets.

A major turning point occurred with the advent of the Industrial Revolution. A dramatically increased amount of convenience foods and inexpensive cooking oils such as corn oil came to market. Our Western diets are full of omega-6s because these oils are cheaper and more stable. Because they prolong the shelf life of processed foods, the food industry replaces healthy fats and oils with ome-

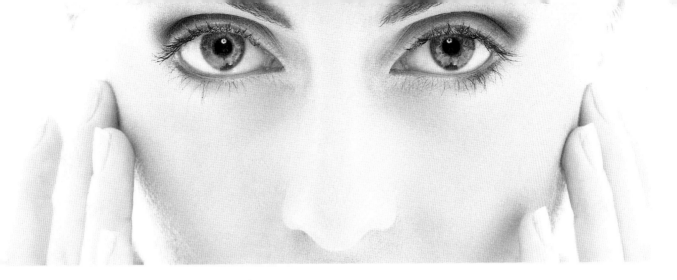

ga-6s and they are to be found hiding in many of the foods we consume. It is therefore no surprise the daily ratio of bad-to-good oil increased each decade since then, meaning that the number got increasingly far from the equal ratio that nature intended for us. Farther from what our DNA has programmed us to deal with.

Given the unhealthy diets that most Americans today consume, it is no surprise that our nation has perhaps the most pro-inflammatory diet of any country—a ratio of roughly 16 or even higher. Each decade, both our ratio of omega-6 to omega-3 fatty acids and our inflammation levels increase. And this trend continues each time we stop for a burger and fries or choose the wrong oil for our "healthy" salads.

The good news is that astonishing studies are emerging, providing us with evidence that the devastating number of diseases associated with chronic inflammation can be decreased by as small a thing as changing the oils in our diets and thereby improving our ratios. I'll mention just one such study of many.

From the Center of Genetics, Nutrition and Health, Washington, 2009: In this secondary prevention study—meaning patients who had already suffered

a cardiovascular event (heart attack, TIA, or stroke)—people switched their unhealthy high-oil ratio diets to a healthy oil ratio. The results were significant. Simply by switching oils, the ratio numbers of study participants improved from roughly 16 to 4. What happened? The research subjects with the lower ratio (around 4) had a 70 percent lower mortality rate than the subjects who kept to their usual Western high-ratio diets.

The problem is that for most Americans, our numbers are way too high (ratios as high as 24 are not uncommon). That's far, far away from what nature intended for us. But as you'll soon see, it's easy to improve our ratios. Not only can we replace the oils in our pantries, we can incorporate high-quality omega-3 supplements from fish and flax seed oils into our diets. In fact many doctors feel that fish oil supplements are vitally important to incorporate into our healthcare regimens. A supplement high in omega-3s will have a huge effect on your numbers, even if you do slip up and have that occasional donut or bag of fries.

Researchers have discovered that supplements and an oil switch can have profound effects on skin aging as well. These effects take place deep inside your skin—the place where wrinkles are born.

A 2005 study presented in the *Journal of Lipid Research* examined the effects on skin of a diet rich in the healthy omega-3 fatty acids. Experts weren't really sure at the time what to expect. But It was found that EPA, an omega-3 found in fish oil, not only provided hydration by regulating oil function in the body, but it also inhibited one of the most destructive agers of our skin in the first place: MMPs, the enzymes that eat away at our dermal safety net. These culprits, which are activated by the sun, are one of the biggest offenders—leading to wrinkles and loss of elasticity. The less they become activated to do their dirty work, the younger your skin will remain.

IT'S AN EASY CHOICE

Switch your cooking oil. Olive oil is a good choice because it is low in omega-6. If you don't choose olive oil, canola oil is a close second. Avoid at all costs partially hydrogenated oils, peanut oil, soybean oil, corn oil, and regular sunflower and safflower oil.

Consider supplements of fish oil, krill oil, and flax-seed oil. There probably is no faster or easier way to change your ratio for the better.

ASK THE
EXPERT

Dr. Wendy Roberts

Well-equipped by the rigors of her Stanford Medical School training, surgical and dermatology residences, followed by a Pathology fellowship. Dr. Roberts was the Founding Director of Dermatopathology of Loma Linda Division of Dermatology. Her innovative methods have earned her national and international recognition. She developed the Roberts Skin Type Classification System© which is a comprehensive scale to classify all skin types. She was awarded a trademark for developing Generational Dermatology™ which is a multi-decade approach to the evolving aging patient. She has been voted by her physician peers as a "Best Doctor" by Palm Springs Life magazine in 2005, 2006, 2007, 2008, 2009, 2010, 2011, 2012, 2013, and 2014. Dr. Roberts' private practice is based in Rancho Mirage, California. As a key opinion leader for dermatology her medical expertise is embraced by skin experts, the pharmaceutical industry, patients, and medical colleagues worldwide.

Q: Dr. Roberts, now that my readers are familiar with the term inflammation and its link to the aging process, I hope that you wouldn't mind sharing your expertise about a prevalent inflammatory condition not necessarily linked to aging, but hugely important to my readers. That would be post-inflammatory hyperpigmentation, or in plain English, the dark spots and discoloration many women of color struggle with. What is it, and why does it occur?

A: Post-inflammatory hyperpigmentation (PIH) is a common inflammatory response of the skin. It tends to affect individuals most commonly of African,

Asian, Pacific Islander, Hispanic, and Indian decent. It is common in mixed populations as well. It is a pigmentation that follows an injury or an inflammatory disorder. PIH may be temporary or permanent, It typically manifests in a pattern of distribution mirroring the inflammatory process. Skin infections, UV insult, burns, drug eruptions from medications, inflammatory conditions such as acne, eczema, psoriasis, as well as many others may trigger the "melanin cascade" which includes excess production of melanin and an excess transfer of the melanin into the surrounding epidermal cells called keratinocytes. Excess melanin may also occur in the deeper dermis and we will discuss later in greater detail.

Q: In your previous interviews, you've mentioned that PIH is much more prevalent for individuals of specific backgrounds. Let's talk about ethnicity and the possibility of developing a condition of PIH. Can you give us more information?

A: There are structural and functional differences in skin of color. Skin environment is also a factor. For example, heat against the skin which does not actually burn the skin may result in PIH. Being aware of the link between your heritage and preponderance of developing PIH is tremendously important. For example, let's have a look at the prevalence of developing PIH post acne. This would mean that after an acne lesion (pimple) has resolved, the patient would be left with a dark spot in place of the lesion. A 2002 study evaluating the PIH development post acne found that 63% of African Americans, 52.7% of Hispanics, and 47.4% of Asians will develop this condition. Persons of mixed heritage, for example

Caucasian and African American, may have skin reactions similar to either parent or a mix of both.

If patients have better understanding about the role PIH plays in relationship to acne and other skin conditions, they can experience much better outcomes. For example, they need to be particularly careful when treating their acne. Some treatments can actually worsen their condition—an example would be "squeezing the pimple" in an effort to remove the visible head. Time is also a factor. The management of PIH starts with addressing the underlying inflammatory condition and in the case of acne, it must be treated as early as possible. The acne must first be eliminated and treated before the PIH can effectively be prevented. Every time a new acne lesion develops and resolves a new area of discoloration may develop. It is absolutely crucial to minimize outbreaks with appropriate medications because only then can treatment for PIH be effective. This will hasten its resolution and prevent further darkening.

Q: Thanks for that important advice. It appears that education is key. Because there is a huge link between ethnic background and preponderance of developing PIH, you would think that we would learn more about this condition in the media, yet there is a lack of press on this topic.
You've been a pioneer in this field and getting the word out! In fact, you've developed a newer, better skin classification scale called the Roberts Skin Type Classification System©. It is being touted as a much more realistic and effective tool to ensure the right treatments are performed on the right people. In other words, it would ensure better outcomes for cosmetic procedures and treatments. Can you tell us more?

A: Yes, in the past, skin types were classified using what is called the Fitzpatrick Skin Type Scale. It is simple, widely used, and user friendly, yet fails to accurately predict the skins response to injury and insult from cosmetic and non-cosmetic procedures such as skin biopsy or acne extractions. The Fitzpatrick scale classifies individuals based upon tendency to burn or tan from UV rays. My scale incorporates newer research about the correlation between ethnicity and tendency to develop PIH. It can be a predictor of an individual's risk for impending complications such as hyperpigmentation and scarring, which can then be avoided. Let me give your readers an example. If a physician sees a patient who has a lighter-colored complexion, he or she might think it safe to proceed with a specific strength peel or laser treatment. The treatment is given, and to your surprise, that patient has developed PIH complications. If the doctor had pre-screened using my scale, a pre-treatment spot test could have been performed that would determine safety and tolerance. The patient would have been spared from the serious complications.
In evaluating patient's skin and developing a cosmetic plan my scale includes 4 key factors: 1) propensity for hyper/hypopigmentation risk, 2) scarring risk, 3) skin photo type (Fitzpatrick scale) and 4) skin photo age type (Glogau). All combined are critical indicators that ensure optimal outcomes and safety.

Q: That is vital information for my readers. Next, I need to ask, are there any lifestyle changes that can prevent or protect from worsening of this condition?

A: Probably the number-one lifestyle change would be to limit unprotected sun exposure. Sun protection is an integral part of treatment and should never be overlooked or underestimated. Just because an individual isn't likely to develop a burn from UV exposure doesn't indicate that it's safe for that person to sunbathe. It's a fact, all ethnicities can and will suffer sun damage. Human skin has a natural built in SPF which ranges from 0-13 depending on melanin content. The highest number SPF 13 is not a great amount of sun protection. Any UV exposure fuels the condition of PIH. Climactic evolution with ozone depletion is also a contributing factor. Sun exposure no matter how little or great will preferentially darken the areas of PIH. People should use a broad-spectrum SPF and reapply throughout the day.

Q: What's the difference between epidermal PIH and deeper, dermal PIH? And, what does it mean to the average person?

A: Epidermal PIH tends to appear tan, brown, or dark brown. It can take months to years to resolve without treatment. Dermal PIH—because it's deeper and more permanent—may have a dark brown or blue-grey appearance and is much more difficult to treat.

Q: Is dermal PIH one of the reasons topical treatments have little effect?

A: Yes, PIH within the dermis results from the release of melanin from the epidermal cells into the deeper-located inflammatory cells called macrophages. These cells essentially engulf the melanin and become melanophages. They reside in the upper dermis where it can become permanent or semi-permanent. In any case, dermal PIH because of its location both within the inflammatory cell and within the deeper dermis is much more difficult to treat.

Q: How about treatments such as microdermabrasion, chemical peels, or laser resurfacing?

A. For the treatment of PIH, resurfacing treatments can be effective alone for superficial PIH and even more effective if used in conjunction with effective topicals. Roberts Skin Type Classification© should be elicited when selecting combination peels and treatments to avoid irritation which can worsen PIH and lead to other complications. Some cases of PIH, such as dermal PIH, will require laser treatment if a combination of topicals and peels have failed.

Q: Thanks for all this great information, Dr. Roberts. I would be remiss if I didn't ask you the most important reason anyone with dark spots and/or discoloration should see a dermatologist.

A: First you want to make sure the dark spot is not a skin cancer or another skin disorder such as cutaneous lupus or sarcoidosis. No matter how "skin savvy" a person is, he or she doesn't have the trained eyes and sensitive instruments to identify skin cancers. Always seek out a diagnosis from a skilled dermatologist before you decide to treat your dark spots on your own. Please remember, stay out of sun, daily use of broad spectrum SPF, antioxidants, and always be gentle with your skin. Also, understand that the dermatologists of today have access to much better treatment modalities than they did years ago.

HORMONES

04

REASON #4 • HORMONES

Hormones are often referred to as the body's chemical messengers. As vital as hormones are to the body, they have a major impact on skin, and shifts in hormone levels are responsible for many of the changes you see as you age. Your skin is not only a target organ for many hormones—estrogen, testosterone, DHEA, and vitamin D, to name a few—new research has shown that it has the ability to produce hormones by itself and can even be considered an independent peripheral endocrine organ. From regulating metabolism and growth to controlling immune function and reproduction, hormones are major players in the human body.

There has been a plethora of research into how to harness the power of hormones to slow the general aging process. Both men and women are taking a close look at hormone levels to ensure a better quality of life as they age. But just how important are hormones to the aging process of skin?

Think of hormones as a central command, issuing out instructions for your skin to function and produce things. Your hormone levels will determine how thick your skin is, how much oil is produced by your skin,

how many water-holding cells it contains, how much collagen your skin will maintain, and much more. Hormones exert their effects on skin through interaction with highly specific receptors found on the cells. Think of receptors as tiny doors with locks, often located on the exterior of cells, waiting for a specific key to bind with it. When a specific lock (cell receptor) and key (hormone) are paired, the commands from the hormone are given to the cell and it fires into action. Hormones aren't the only substances that bind to skin cell receptors and fire your skin into action. You'll read about other key players elsewhere in this book.

WHEN SKIN CELLS SLOW DOWN

What happens as we age is that our hormone levels decrease. Once the levels of hormones decrease, cells just don't receive as many commands to do things and your skin slows down on just about every level. Of particular concern are women who experience menopause. Because they experience a tremendous drop in estrogen levels, within five years of menopause, 30 percent of collagen is lost.

Experts attribute the loss of collagen to the wrinkles menopausal women experience. What's more, there are a preponderance of estrogen receptors found on facial skin, making this skin particularly susceptible to the consequences of estrogen depletion.

The loss of hormones during menopause is responsible for a restructuring of fat deposits in the body that have their own impact on facial appearance. As estrogen levels drop during menopause, fat deposits throughout the body tend to become reattributed away from the face, neck, and hands—into the abdomen, thighs, and buttocks. The result is a loss of supportive fat below the skin of the face, neck, and hands resulting in the appearance of sagging wrinkles. The skin over these areas becomes less easily compressed and loses its mobility.

The growth and maintenance of your skin's capillaries are also under the control of estrogens. This effect contributes to the thinning of skin. When estrogen is diminished, bloodflow through the dermal capillaries is reduced. The result is that less nutrients and oxygen are available to the living layer of the epidermis. This contributes to its thinning and to a slower turnover rate which is accompanied by an impaired barrier function. The result? Skin loses water content or moisture more easily, and it becomes drier.

But hold on, there's more to the story. Not only do women have to deal with a tremendous loss in collagen—about a 30 percent drop—as well as the drying effects, overall thinning, and shifting of fat deposits from the face to the abdomen, but new research points to loss of estrogen playing a key role in accelerating the one primary environmental factor that spells aging skin. That's the sun. Estrogen loss accelerates the rate of enzyme activation that destroys the dermal elastin network. Menopausal women are especially vulnerable to the damaging effect UV rays can have on their skin.

IS HRT THE ANSWER?

Our thoughts often turn to hormone replacement therapy as the rational answer. Needless to say, women don't request hormone replacement because they are worried about their skin's appearance, but rather they request it because they are looking for relief. We know that hormone replacement therapy provides relief from poor sleep patterns, hot flashes, mood swings, and a general loss of well-being. In fact, many of us may feel like we're running on empty, merely going through the motions of life. Improvement in the youthfulness of our skin would be viewed as a side benefit to having one's quality of life back—like the icing on the cake.

But, unfortunately, it isn't quite that simple. There has been a major breaking point in the practice of prescribing hormones for the alleviation of menopausal symptoms, particularly estrogen and progesterone. This break occurred early in 2002, when the result of a wide-ranging study by the name of the Women's Health Initiative (WHI) were announced. In a nutshell, while the study was designed to conclude that hormone therapy could prevent heart attacks, doctors hypothesized that the increase in heart attacks seen in menopausal women was actually partially caused by decreasing hormone levels. This sadly wasn't the case. In fact, according to the study, heart problems were significantly increased in the population of women who took HRT, along with an increase in cancers.

ARE WOMEN HEARING THE WHOLE STORY?

Many are questioning the study's conclusions, wondering if the increase in adverse side effects were due to the hormonal increases administered for the study, or if they were due to the integrity of the hormones themselves (women were given synthetic hormones in levels that may have been much higher than necessary). Many women today are wondering if there are safer alternatives.

Fortunately, there are.

Enter the age of bioidentical hormones, which are what many believe to be a safe alternative to HRT. Bioidentical hormones are hormones created from plants, and they are believed to be chemically identical to the hormones produced by the human endocrine system during youth. What's more, these hormones are administered in a way that mimics the body's natural production of hormones. Because they are applied topically in a cream or gel formulation, they are released into the bloodstream without first having to pass through the stomach and liver. This makes their administration much more predictable and precise.

The entire concept of naturally derived bioidentical hormones has been hugely maligned by the press, as well as much of the medical community. The opposing side to bioidentical hormones make the case that hormones, whether created from horse urine or plants, are still hormones. Because they are equal to each other, the only "sensible" conclusion is that hormones in any form would share similar side effect profiles and increase cancer rates. I feel that because of this thought process, they have turned a blind eye to the European safety data which clearly demonstrates that plant-derived hormones are not only safe, but beneficial in actually lowering some cancer rates.

However, proponents of bioidentical compounds feel there are significant differences between the two. A major difference is an alteration of the pharmaceutical estrogen hormone, which is derived from horse urine, to have it qualify for a patent. Because the hormone molecule is tweaked in an effort to generate a patent, it is not completely identical to the natural hormones that our body creates. Endorsers of plant-derived hormones conclude that this practice alone might explain the dangerous side effects of synthetic hormones. This slight difference is critical to its structure, and may lead to unnecessary stimulating and mutating effects on the breast and uterus.

Whatever the truth is, because of this mass fear of traditional estrogen use, millions of women are now suffering from overwhelming menopausal symptoms, a devastating effect on skin being just one of those symptoms.

Because of this controversy, I considered not even including bioidentical hormones in my book...but this book is about what actually works for skin. While many topicals can be greatly beneficial, no topical is going to bring your skin back to the vitality and brilliance of your youth the way that hormone replacement will. While we learned in this chapter that hormone replacement will not reverse sun damage, many studies document that it can prevent a drastic downhill slide, as well as recoup much of the loss— even when HRT is taken many years after the start of menopause.

Certainly, the conversation needs to continue, and people like Suzanne Somers should be applauded. Suzanne has had to withstand a barrage of criticism from much of the medical community for her decisions on HRT. The reality is simple, most women who get their hormones balanced seem to say the same thing: "It's one of the best decisions I've ever made." I'm one of these people.

Because of this, I've included in this book an age breaker interview with a pioneering physician and author Dr. Selma Rashid who specializes in bioidentical hormone therapy. I want you, the reader, to be able to better empower yourself on this vital topic.

Dr. Selma Rashid

Leading Expert in Bioidentical Hormone
Replacement Therapy

Born in the UK, Dr. Selma Rashid, M.D. completed her medical degree and training in Chicago, Illinois. Dr. Rashid is board-certified in Internal Medicine. Now an acknowledged global expert on hormone replacement therapy, she recognizes that it has become increasingly confusing for the lay public— as well as healthcare providers—due to years of circulating misinformation. Dr. Rashid is dedicated to clarifying the truth, so people can make informed decisions based on well-established facts.
As an academic and scientist, she strives to help the medical profession think outside the constraints of standard medicine, and draw medical knowledge from sound scientific data for the benefit of the patient, and not be limited by stale practices or those backed by financial interests. Through her presentations to public groups, as well as her top-selling book, Hormones Explained, *Dr. Selma Rashid also enables people to make more intelligent and educated health choices.*

Q: Dr. Rashid, everyone is hearing about and talking about hormones these days. Because you are one of the country's experts in this field, can you share the following with my readers? They are very interested in the link between hormones and diseases, osteoporosis, depression, and finally, skin aging.

On age-related diseases:

Estradiol and Progesterone are produced in a distinct cyclical pattern during our fertile years. The years of fertility are the healthiest years of our lives. Estradiol and Progesterone are powerful steroid hormones, and act on almost every cell in our body, as well as optimize the function of many other important hormone systems. We are designed to decline in health and eventually die. In women, the diminishing levels and eventual loss of Estradiol and Progesterone, triggers the accelerated rate of aging.

Brain function and cognition are directly related to the effects of Estradiol. Bone health is dependent on Estradiol. Estradiol facilitates cholesterol getting into our cells and become the many essential molecules that we need for a healthy nervous system; it also enhances the function of Insulin and helps thyroid hormones to work better. Many studies over decades have demonstrated how important Estradiol and Progesterone are on the cardiovascular system, but sadly, the WHI used the wrong hormones in the wrong way, which caused many problems. As a result, mainstream medicine rejected Estradiol and Progesterone for cardiovascular protection, taking us decades backwards.

On osteoporosis and bone health:

Estradiol is necessary for bone health. Bone constantly remodels, and Estradiol plays a key role in the process. A decline in Estradiol is directly linked to osteopenia and osteoporosis, which leads to increased risk of fractures. Inadequate bone remodeling contributes to loss of height by compression of the spine, as well as increasing back pain.

On the link between hormones and depression:

A woman who was handling life well, and develops symptoms of depression at perimenopause, menopause or after childbirth, must have hormone imbalance ruled out before reaching for antidepressants. Without doubt, a woman who does not ovulate well will not produce adequate amounts of Progesterone and will have "mood" symptoms. She will almost definitely have an inadequate response to emotional triggers. For example, she may experience more frustration, impatience, tearfulness, bouts of unjustified rage, anger, guilt, impending doom, sadness, anxiety, depressed, short fuse, etc. Everyone reacts differently, but it's all linked to the same deficit and treated the same way. Antidepressants alter brain chemicals in an unnatural way. Hormone restoration addresses mood imbalance in a biological way.

On the link between hormones and skin aging:

Estradiol has easy access into just about every cell, and once it gets in, it signals the cells to do what they are designed to do. Skin cells make collagen and elastic tissue among many other essential components of a healthy radiant skin. Women who are Estrogen balanced have a youthful glow, something that menopausal women definitely begin to lose.

Q: You are passionate about preventing diseases and dysfunctions of aging. You also found the traditional standard of care approach lacking. What led you to pursue a different path of medicine that focuses on prevention?

A: I also work as a Hospitalist in acute care medicine, and see the direct results of aging, and the diseases that come along with it. Mainstream medicine disregards true preventive medicine. Hospitals profit enormously from the diseases of aging, such as hip fracture and heart disease, for example. With surgical procedures, hospital profits multiply by magnitudes. These incredible profits that hospitals enjoy, drive medical insurance costs higher and higher. In this generation, consumers will have to take charge of educating themselves on true prevention. I see how difficult it is for consumers to know what to do, who to listen to, or who to believe. For those who are truly seeking answers, I love to be able to provide an overview of our options, based on true medical science.

Q: Now let's get to probably the number one reason mainstream medicine has discarded HRT as a viable option for prevention of many diseases. That's the WHI study. As a reminder to our readers, in 2002 the WHI, Women's Health Initiative, released the results of a ten-year study into the effects of conventional HRT on women's bodies. In your book you go into great detail to highlight glaring discrepancies. In fact, they are alarming to read about! Can you tell my readers a little about these?

A: This is a very important issue, and women are going to have to understand this clearly, as their doctors for the most part have decided not to.

The study showed NO link between Estrogen and breast cancer. In one group of the study, only estrogen vs. placebo was given. The study was stopped early because of an increase in blood clots, not because of any increase in cancer. Several years later, the women who only received estrogen were found to have LESS breast cancer than the placebo group.

In the Estrogen/Progestin (note, NOT Progesterone) group, there was more breast cancer compared to the placebo. It was very clear that the Progestin was the culprit. Our bodies own Progesterone is well known to protect our breasts, but the synthetic form (Progestin), had been previously documented to increase the risk of breast cancer.

Again, the only difference in the two hormone study groups was, one had only estrogen, the other had estrogen and progesterone. It was the group that had estrogen and progesterone that was shown to have more breast cancer.

Note: The medical establishment clearly recognizes that prior to the WHI study, there was NO link of Estrogen to breast cancer or heart disease. In fact, the scientific literature hailed the benefits of Estrogen and Progesterone. If there were any doubts, 30,000 women would not have been subjected to hormones remotely suspected to cause harm. This study was funded by our government, designed by our top scientists/physicians, and managed in the top clinical centers in the country. Thus, we can be assured that prior to this study, Estrogen was not linked to breast cancer. What these elite group of people did not pay attention to, was that synthetic progesterone was already known to be linked to breast cancer, and ANY Estrogen by mouth will increase the risk of blood clots, which we unfortunately saw in the form of strokes, heart attacks, and lung clots (pulmonary embolism).

(This study was a national embarrassment. Many women suffered from the study, and many more continue to suffer due to the misrepresentation of the results and the continuing ignorance.)

Wow, thanks Dr. Rashid, for a wealth of important information. Knowledge is indeed powerful!

GLYCATION

04

REASON #5 • GLYCATION

Who doesn't love sugar? We've been trained to associate sugars and starches with many different blissful milestones in life. Sugar reminds us of that beautiful birthday or wedding cake, a graduation, an anniversary. Candy canes, cookies, and all kinds of tempting treats are staples for most of us during the holidays, and we give and receive these items in the spirit of love and friendship without realizing the havoc sugar is wreaking on our bodies.

SUGAR IS BECOMING PUBLIC ENEMY #1

Most of us are aware of the negative consequences of elevated sugar levels. They cause diseases such as diabetes and heart disease, and they harm blood vessels and nerve endings. But did you know that sugars have been named a major villain causing hardening of arteries? So much has been discovered about the link between sugar and arteries that the American Heart Association has recommended no more than 100 calories per day of sugar for women, and 150 calories per day for men.

So why does this happen, and what's the connection between sugar and skin?

When you consume sugar, it undergoes a non-enzymatic process called glycation. Glycation happens when sugars attach to proteins and form a sticky molecule. This molecule goes deep into your youth zone and gums it up, finding the place in your skin with the most protein—your perfect, wonderful safety net of collagen and elastin. When weakened, that net is responsible for the deep wrinkles that we all want to avoid. It's like launching a hot tar warfare campaign—these sticky molecules make the safety net stiff and cause breakage. Because collagen fibers have such a long half life, the jury is still out as to whether the damage done by sugar is permanent or reversible.

BY AGE 35

Glycation causes changes in everyone's skin by middle age. A 2007 study in the *British Journal of Dermatology* highlighted that glycation's destruction of collagen and elastin takes hold by age 35. Scientists can even measure the amount of glycation using sophisticated Visia complexion-analysis cameras that show glycation as a high florescence.

Have you noticed that your skin has lost its luminosity, whether dark or fair, by age 35? If you have a diet high in sugar, your skin will tend to have a more-yellowed color to it, losing its pureness and clarity of color. There's a reason why smokers' skin is particularly yellowish in appearance. This is a consequence of the body's depletion of vitamin C and E which is a result of smoking. These vitamins are the body's way of fighting off glycation's harmful effects. Smokers are at a huge disadvantage when it comes to having a brilliant complexion.

BY AGE 60+

Some experts believe that the older you are, the more you should be concerned with the detrimental effects of consuming too many sugars and starches. The reason is that when we get older, we produce less and less collagen and elastin, the prime target of AGEs. Because your skin's manufacturing plant produces less, you need to do what you can to protect your current inventory of collagen and elastin. If your inventory of collagen fibers gets damaged, you are stuck with the damage for a longer period of time.

The good news is that like many causes of aging, glycation can be controlled, and many believe that it can even be partially reversed. The firmness and texture of your skin's support structure can be refined through several different means. Sugar bonds can be reversed, and collagen production can be increased. There is a way that your skin's youthful color can be restored, and your skin can become more firm and resilient. Please refer to your Skin Pearls Glossary for a list of today's glycation inhibitors.

1. HEALTHY COLLAGEN

In the dermis, healthy elastin and collagen fibers are the protein structures that keep our skin firm and smooth. Young skin is free of the aging effects of glycation.

2. HIGH CARB DIET

Termed the Maillard Reaction, as blood sugar levels rise, the sugars attach themselves in a haphazard way to the peptide chains in the collagen and elastin fibers. As this occurs, the skin proteins become stiff and less subtle.

3. COLLAGEN DESTRUCTION

Over time, rigid bonds develop between fibers causing brittleness and breakage. The sugars also diminish skin's vascular and fibroblast activity in a similar manner.

THINGS YOU SHOULD KNOW ABOUT

We are all familiar with self-tanners. They generate a non-melanin browning (tanning) of our epidermal skin. These products contain reducing molecules, the most widely used ingredient being dihydroxy-acetone (DHA), a simple carbohydrate. It is often derived from plant sources such as sugar beets and sugar cane. These carbohydrates undergo a Maillard reaction with skin-surface proteins. They react with cornified dead cells and produce a golden brown color. The color remains durable until the stratum corneum cells are removed by grad-ual shedding. However, it has been reported that a portion of the ingredients will penetrate deeper, reaching living epidermal and dermal cells where they promote protein glycation, one of the principal aging mechanisms.

"Bottom line – Experts are still undecided about the safety of self-tanners. You may want to save yours for special occasions like a wedding or a hot date!"

Age Breakers

BREAK THE BONDS THAT AGE

Besides cutting down on sugars and starches in your diet, nature has provided us with powerful allies in the quest for beautiful skin. Studies show that certain foods may serve as inhibitors in the destructive process of glycation. For example, carnosine, found in health food stores, not only appears to prevent the reaction but undo some of the glycation damage deep inside the dermis.

Certain plant extracts have also been studied for their potential to prevent glycation. Among those that have shown promising results are cinnamon, black pepper, ginger, cumin, and green tea. Cinnamon has become a front runner in the war against glycation and intakes of even small amounts appear to be effective. However, stay clear of "mock cinnamons" such as Cassia which has significant amounts of coumarin which can be toxic to the kidneys. Invest in true cinnamon, which is Ceylon cinnamon.

Vitamin B has three forms. Look for pyridoxamine, the third form. Supplementation with this form of vitamin B6 has a proven track record for inhibiting the glycation process.

You may look at vinegar in a whole new way. Several studies have shown that it will lower blood sugar levels even after a starchy meal. Yeah!

QUICK AND EASY DIETARY INCLUSIONS TO HELP BREAK THE BONDS AND SAVE YOUR SKIN:

- GINGER
- CUMIN
- GREEN TEA
- CINNAMON
- VITAMIN B6

Age Breakers
THE FAST LANE TO AGING SKIN

Wrinkles and slackness in the skin are an outward manifestation of the oxidation and glycation that is also happening inside your body. Eating a diet high in sugar is definitely not a good idea. However did you know that eating a diet containing fructose is 10 times more likely to glycate and damage skin than glucose? More than any other ingredient available for consumption, excess fructose has been proven in numerous studies to accelerate aging of the skin. It not only promotes formation of AGEs, it is extremely pro-inflammatory.

Even in small amounts, there is potential for damage to your skin.

Not only does fructose age skin 10 times more that glucose, researchers have discovered that consuming fructose even in large amounts doesn't suppress hunger. It causes ghrelin, a hunger hormone, to rise. As a result, your brain perceives it is still hungry so it is natural to continue eating even well after consuming the calories you actually need.

This fast lane to aging, high-fructose syrup has crept up in our American diets. The average American eats 35 pounds of high-fructose corn syrup per year. Because it is present in over 90% of processed food items like sodas and candy, it is easy to see how the average American can consume large quantities.

Ever wonder the secret to the A lister star's perfect skin? According to a dermatologist to the stars, they are moving away from fillers and cosmetic procedures that are too obvious. The newer trend is to actually take care of their skin. A crucial part of this new trend is the avoidance of the fast track to aging foods referenced above. One of the most stunning, stars, Jennifer Aniston, is reported to shun sugars and unrefined carbs and instead embrace low-glycemic carbohydrates, lean proteins and essential fats. Without a doubt her skin-friendly diet may be one of the major reasons she is known for possessing one of the most beautiful bodies in Hollywood. Don't your skin and figure deserve the red carpet treatment?

HERE ARE OTHER COMMON FOODS CONTAINING HIDDEN AMOUNTS OF HIGH AMOUNTS OF FRUCTOSE.

JUICE COCKTAILS

If a juice drink is not made with 100 percent juice, it generally contains a large amount of HFCS.

SODA

Try mixing 100% juices with seltzer or look for soda flavors that include cane sugar.

BREAKFAST CEREAL

Even seemingly healthy breakfast cereals contain HFCS. Read labels carefully.

YOGURT

Seemingly healthy, often it is found that those that contain fruit or other sweeteners are full of fructose. Buy plain yogurt and sweeten it with fresh fruit.

SALAD DRESSINGS

High-fructose corn syrup is added to seemingly un-sweet items. Whenever possible, make your own salad dressings. They're easy and more delicious.

BREADS AND BAKED GOODS

The label may say Whole Grain and Healthy, but if you read the ingredients, HFCS is often one of them.

NUTRITION BARS

Don't let the word nutrition fool you!

Believe it or not, even sodas containing some juice have HFCS. This includes Orangina, a seemingly healthy soda.

Switch to a protein drink. Try Premier Protein, 30g protein, 1g sugar, 160 calories. Need I say more?

Buy plain and add the fruit. It's more filling.

Colorful sugar bombs!

Forget the sandwich. Try soup and salad. You'll feel lighter and just as full.

Make your own dressing. It tastes better!

Opt for an iced coffee or latte if you need a jolt of caffeine.

How can so good be so bad!

Philip Young M.D.

Aesthetic Facial Plastic Surgery Bellevue | Seattle

Philip Young M.D. of Aesthetic Facial Plastic Surgery Bellevue, Seattle is triple board certified by the American Board of Facial Plastic and Reconstructive Surgery, American Board of Otolaryngology. Head and Neck Surgery, and the American Board of Laser Surgery. He is an award-winning facial plastic surgeon and published author with a ground-breaking new theory on facial beauty called the Circles of Prominence. He is also proud of scoring the number-one score on the written exam for his board certification by the American Board of Facial Plastic and Reconstructive Surgery.

Q: Dr. Young, could you please shed some light on the role glycation plays in the aging process?

A: Many factors can influence skin aging. These include pollution, UV rays, and cigarette smoke to name a few. However, recent studies have focused on nutrition as an environmental factor that also plays a big role in how your skin ages. Just as a diet high in added sugars and unrefined carbohydrates can lead to the development of such diseases as metabolic syndrome and type II diabetes, the same type of diet can have an impact on your skin's health.

Q: Earlier in my book, I explained what the process of glycation entails—essentially a non-enzymatic process that permanently bonds a sugar to a protein. In the case of our skin, the protein undergoing this transformation is our collagen, the one protein that keeps our skin firm and wrinkle free. Now that my readers understand what goes on internally, could you elaborate on the visual consequences of a sugary diet?

A: Yes. In your mid-thirties glycation affects both collagen and elastin. This is because its visual effects are cumulative. Environmental factors such as sun exposure accelerate the glycation process. It is now believed that the yellowy appearance of actinically damaged skin is due in part to the glycated collagen and elastin network.

Q: Is there any advice you can give the readers to prevent its occurrence?

A: Unfortunately, current research points to the belief that glycated collagen and elastin cannot be reversed, so prevention is key. And there are emerging cosmaceuticals, that may play a role in inhibiting sugar attaching to the proteins in your skin. Products such as plant and algae extracts have been studied in vitro for their potentially beneficial anti-glycation effects.

Q: Dr. Young. Would you please explain to our readers what the term in vitro means?

A: In vitro means that the substance has been studied in a test lab, often times a petri dish or test tube instead of a living person. In vitro results do not always translate to what's called "in vivo"—results that quantify efficacy for a living, breathing person.

Q: OK. Tell us a little about the botanical extracts that may help inhibit the irreversible process of glycation.

A: Probably one of the most researched anti-glycation botanicals is green tea. Animal studies confirm that ingestion can block some of the glycation process. Green tea is well known as a powerful anti-oxidant and may even offer some protection against UV-induced inflammation.

Q: What about other botanicals? Are there any others we should include in our diets?

A: Yes, the substance quercetin, similar to green tea, has broad biologic activity. It is found in your red and blue foods that include red apples, red grapes, red onions, and some berries. Quercetin is now available in some skincare products, but please keep in mind that well-designed clinical studies are still lacking.

Q: Dr. Young, this book obviously is about the skin's aging process and how to topically treat and reverse it, but many of my readers may be considering more advanced options for regaining a more youthful appearance. Certainly, one of the first considerations for choosing a plastic surgeon is finding a doctor who understands facial beauty. You've been internationally recognized with the prestigious Sir Harold Delf Gillies award for your ground-breaking theory on beauty. Please tell us more.

A: Understanding what makes a face beautiful is essential in developing the goals that plastic surgeons strive for when they help their clients. After years of training and practicing in Los Angeles, I noticed that many results that were seen in Hollywood stars were less than optimal. I strongly felt that there was room for improvement. As a consequence, I spent several years studying the reasons for this which ultimately culminated in a ground-breaking *Theory on Facial Beauty called the Circles of Prominence*. I was glad my theory was internationally recognized by my peers at the American Academy of Facial Plastic and Reconstructive Surgery who awarded me the Sir Harold Delf Gillies Award in 2005.

Q: Because of this achievement, and many other reasons, you and your team have patients come to you from all around the world, including Syria, Dubai, China, Korea, Japan, Australia, England, Canada, the Netherlands, and Singapore to take advantage of your unique YoungVitalizer.™ Please tell my readers a bit more about this.

A: As you age, you lose volume in your face, which eventually creates a saggy, aging appearance. One way to think of aging is to imagine that your face is a grape and as you age, your face loses volume and resembles a raisin. A facelift takes the extra skin off of the raisin and basically makes it into a smaller raisin, which looks nothing like the original healthy grape. That is where the unnatural effect is often seen when you see the results of today's traditional facelifts. What the raisin really needed was extra volume to make it look younger and more natural again like it did when it was a grape. This same principle applies to a person's face. When we age, we lose youthful volume within our face and plastic surgery has traditionally taken the concept of reductive-type procedures where things are taken away instead of added. Although extra skin, and extra fat could be removed and the appearance improved, a person

often would not look necessarily younger. Many times these traditional approaches would leave people appearing unnatural, hollow and with the operated look. The YoungVitalizer™ is different because it recreates youthful volume within the face to make people look better in a younger and natural way.

My goal was to find a method to bring back a person's natural youthfulness without the operated, unnatural look, and that is why I have my patients bring in photos of them when they were age 5 to 30. My YoungVitalizer™ helps restore natural and youthful contours they haven't seen in years."

With the YoungVitalizer™, dark circles and hollows underneath the eye can be filled in, the folds around the mouth are diminished, and the cheeks can be lifted so they become more youthful and radiant. Instead of excising skin in the upper eyelids and lifting the eyebrows so they look surprised, the YoungVitalizer™ can fill in the upper eye area to bring back natural youthfulness without the operated look. The entire face glows from the natural stimulation and the overall effect is better than a facelift in our opinion and experience. The YoungVitalizer™ can give a person a younger and more natural look without general anesthesia, without the invasiveness of a facelift and often without the price of traditional facelifts.

Q: How can my readers learn more about your YoungVitalizer™?

A: They can visit my web site at DrPhillipYoung.com or YoungVitalizer.com and view a multitude of before and after photos.

Thanks for sharing your expertise with us, Dr Young! You've not only shared your expertise about new insights into glycation and skin aging, but also your forward thinking, ground-breaking developments in the field of plastic surgery. My readers thank you as well!

Chapter 5

WHAT'S MISSING FROM YOUR SKINCARE REGIMEN?

05

DAILY SMOOTHING

Probably the number-one missed opportunity for reversing wrinkled skin and locking it into youth mode is neglecting (or objecting to the concept of) daily exfoliation. Chances are, you need to rid your skin of dead cell buildup on a much more consistent basis than you are probably experiencing now.

While it's true that many of us embrace the concept of a weekly exfoliation scrub or at-home peel—using our Clarisonics when we remember to—or a monthly trip to the spa for a quick microdermabrasion treatment, the very idea of ridding skin of dead, hardened, keratinized cells on a daily basis is considered to be excessive and damaging. Women are just beginning to understand that the exterior of skin, the epidermis, is constantly in a growth mode. It is very active and complex, and it sheds itself of dead cells pushed up from the lowest layers each and every day. In fact, by the age of 70, each of us has lost approximately 40 pounds of skin through the course of our lifetimes as a result of this process. All that dust you see piling up around your house? It is actually composed of about 75 percent dead skin cells.

The problem is that, as we age, our skin's built-in enzyme system responsible for facilitating the removal of dead cells malfunctions—often due to such factors as a lack of hydration—and a buildup of dead skin cells ensues. This buildup of hardened cells is responsible for poor penetration of those expensive anti-agers you bought, as well as other factors researchers are now discovering contribute to wrinkle formation.

CRITICAL DISCOVERIES THAT PAY OFF IN A BIG WAY

As scientists started developing enzymes and other exfoliators to aid in the process of sweeping away dead cell buildup, critical discoveries were being made. Initially, the sole purpose of exfoliation was to uncover the more youthful skin below, giving a quick freshening effect to enjoy. Yet, over a period of time, researchers discovered that the very act itself of ridding the top layer of deadened cells stimulated and even shocked skin deep below the top layer to go into a youth-production mode. They discovered that the dermal layer is secondarily or indirectly

affected by the removal of dead cells on the area above it—the surface of the epithelium termed the stratum corneum.

What was once thought to be only a superficial benefit is now believed to have a major effect on a critical skin zone. Recall in previous chapters that the dermal layer, which can be affected by exfoliating the top layer, is the critical layer where aging takes place. This layer is sometimes referred to as the repair zone by researchers because this is the zone that is perpetually in a repair mode. It is the skin layer where youthful collagen, elastin, capillaries, and moisture-binding cells are either being produced with the end result of diminishing wrinkles, or being broken down with the end result of increasing wrinkles. Remember that col-

lagen production is the foundation of youthful, healthy skin. It supplies thickness and attracts moisture to keep skin fresh, wrinkle-free, taut, and radiant.

Some physicians have even invented curious titles for the anti-aging effects of exfoliation. Some specialists term the act of exfoliation as skin exercising because consistent exfoliation builds up the dermal layer similar to the building and toning of muscles through exercise. Deeper exfoliation by way of intensive peels—using chemicals, TCAs, or laser CO_2—are sometimes referred to as shocking the dermis below because it initiates an extreme repair action by creating much higher levels of the collagen matrix. The deeper the peel, the more time it takes to heal, the more collagen and other ele-

ments produced, and the more dramatic the results for such conditions as sun damage, deep wrinkles, and acne scarring. But a consistent, daily exfoliation has been shown to keep skin functioning in a more-youthful manner without putting skin into a shock mode, but rather by putting it into a youth mode where the fibroblasts are operating at consistently higher levels. The trick is that there is not a one-size-fits-all approach. Some skin types, particularly ethnic skin, need to be exfoliated in a particularly kind and gentle way. More on this later.

WRINKLE WAR!

NEW SCIENTIFIC DISCOVERY - DAILY TOP LAYER STIMULATION INHIBITS WRINKLE CREATION.

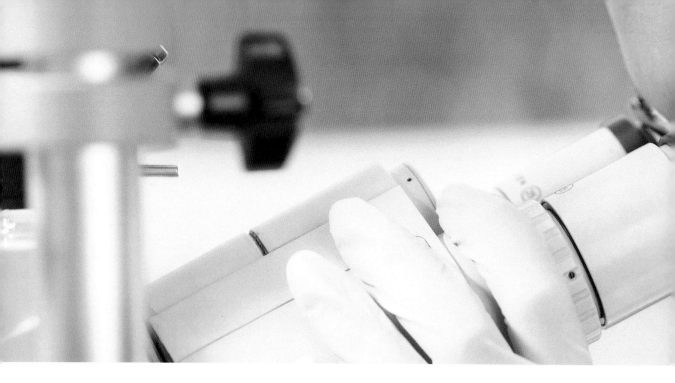

A SKINCARE MAVERICK

It is a well-known fact that in the field of medicine, skincare, and healthcare in general, everyone usually follows carefully planned, standardized methods of treatment for most conditions. Often progress moves slowly as everyone conforms to the standard norm of practice. However, every once in a while an out-of-the-box thinker, or as others may call him or her, a maverick, rises above the rest. I encountered such a maverick—an anti-aging pioneer—some thirty years ago, just as I was entering the medical field of pharmaceuticals and research.

Troubled by my rapidly advancing crow's feet, turkey neck, and uneven skin tone, I actively searched for a new approach

to solve these problems, as my then-current treatment was clearly ineffective. Naturally, I wanted to follow the real science, and not the ineffective marketing gimmicks and trends I encountered while working as a cosmetics salesperson.

Desperate to improve my appearance, I started searching and reading hundreds of medical research papers and articles on the topic of skincare and aging. Eventually, I found what I initially considered to be a shocking article written by a renowned New York City dermatologist. This dermatologist unequivocally claimed that one of the major missing components to the anti-aging skincare regimen was the act of ridding skin of the superficial dead cell buildup using an aggressive daily regimen. Along

with complete shielding from the sun, she herself exfoliated both her face and body each and every day with what most of us would consider to be a highly abrasive grooming tool.

A UNIQUE APPROACH REAPS 3 MAJOR BENEFITS

The dermatologist believed that the anti-aging effects she and many of her patients experienced were three-fold. Number one, it inhibited the formation of corneocyte plugs that top and wedge in wrinkles and creases (refer to the Wrinkle 101 section of this book); number two, it stimulated collagen below the surface as it adjusted to the ever-increasing exfoliating levels; and, number three, it allowed much better penetration of anti-aging treatments.

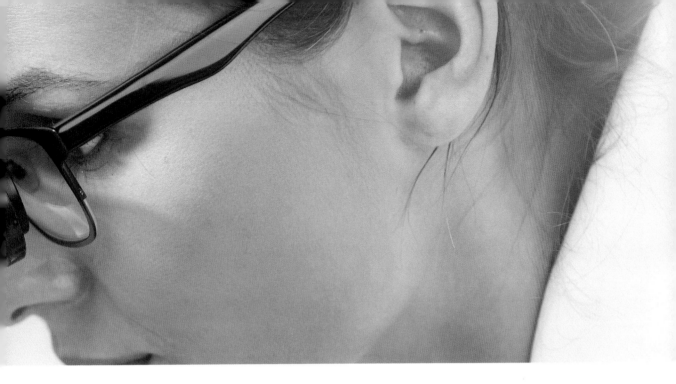

This doctor believed that this method had the profound effect of diminishing current wrinkles while preventing new ones from forming. She attributed this specific method to the unwrinkled, beautiful smooth texture of her own skin, and that of many of her patients. "My skin is my fortune," she stated in one interview. She alluded to receiving negative comments from many in the medical community as daily exfoliation was considered, at the time, to be an extreme action. Yet, upon close inspection of her recommendations, I sensed a logical and sensible skincare plan. Instead of shocking skin, she recommended a method of slowly building higher levels of exfoliation over a lengthy period of time—over weeks or months. She believed that this method ultimately was safe and put the patient in the driver's seat as they were slowly building tolerance to the manual exfoliation process, while at the same time, not exposing skin to the harsh enzymes and acids contained in many chemical peels.

ANY RATIONAL PERSON READING THIS DOCTOR'S ARTICLE WOULD SEE THE ELEPHANT IN THE ROOM

The men and shaving connection—that is, the fact that men who shave daily using a razor have unwrinkled skin in the shaven places. Some skincare specialists try to manufacture a problem that men's skin is under constant abuse by the extreme exfoliation of the razor blade, and as a consequence, is aging rapidly due to the inflammation that shaving most likely triggers. Aside from occasional razor bumps, it's difficult to find men with significant signs of aging in the area they shave. Although this physician did not recommend anything as extreme as using a razor blade, common knowledge makes the connection that daily shaving is daily exfoliating.

At the time, when I was just beginning to study medical science, her recommendation of daily exfoliation sounded sensible, logical, and, doable to me, so I gave her method a try. I trusted her recommendation to start the process with a simple washcloth, and over weeks and months, I built the intensity of the process by using gentle pH-balanced cleansers along with various exfoliation pads, making sure

to keep them clean and sterile. As weeks went by, I slowly increased the intensity of the pad. Without a doubt, it was a transformative process to my skin and to my appearance. Thirty years later, while working as an esthetician, I had the wonderful opportunity to recommend this method to my clients whose major concerns were wrinkles. The results spoke for themselves. The many thank yous I received from my clients was tremendously gratifying.

AFTER READING THE ABOVE, YOU MAY REMAIN SKEPTICAL

You may still feel that daily exfoliating may be ultimately harmful and too rough for your skin. It hardly needs to be stated that a healthy, functioning skin barrier is extremely important for skin health, as it is your body's main defense against the environment. It is the body's protector against dehydration, allergens, and penetration against various organisms and general irritants. If skin is over-exfoliated, the lipid levels may be diminished and the barrier may become compromised.

When many of us think of exfoliation, we often think of alpha hydroxy acids. Certain acids have extremely powerful effects on breaking apart the glue-like mortar that holds the wall of dead, keratinized cells together. But they can be tricky to use and that's the reason why most experts do not recommend them for daily use. The reason for this is that embracing a chemical exfoliant as your prime mechanism for a daily smoothing treatment is extremely tricky business. Let's take a closer look at alpha hydroxy acids.

YOU NEED JUST THE RIGHT PERCENTAGE OF ALPHA HYDROXY ACIDS (AHAS) TO BE EFFECTIVE

Around four percent. In addition, the pH has to be in an effective range, around three to five percent. If it's too acidic, your skin will sting and burn—too alkaline, and the exfoliator will be neutralized. If it's not left on your skin long enough, it will not have any substantial exfoliating effect. Save your alpha hydroxy acids to use as a backup anti-ager. There is a wealth of evidence as to the anti-aging benefits

you can derive—please refer to your Skin Pearls Glossary. Just don't rely on a chemical exfoilant, weak or strong, to effectively remove the hardened, dry, dead cells standing between you and a younger appearance. You want controllability from the get go.

ONE SIZE DOESN'T FIT ALL APPROACH

I had also mentioned that there is no one-size-fits-all approach to this method. Ethnic, darker-skinned types are prone to inflammatory problems and may develop hyperpigmentation with something as harmless as a buff puff. Specialists state that this is an extremely difficult condition to repair. Are you prone to this condition? Any skin type that has discoloration or darkened spots from a simple scratch or pimple is often the one prone to this hypersensitive inflammatory condition. However, nature can be kind to ethnic, darker-skinned types, as lucky for them, they do not experience nearly as much of the outward effects of aging that lighter skinned people do. Although they can still also suffer from UV damage and skin cancers, due to a variety of factors they are not prone to unsightly lines, fur-

rows, and the creppiness of their Western European counterparts. Gentle acids are recommended for their skin-smoothing powers for ethnic/darker skin—lactic acid especially will diminish the ashiness that ethnic or darker-skinned people experience from dead cell buildup.

WHAT WORKS AND WHAT DOESN'T?

THE ANSWERS

There is a second piece to the puzzle of what's missing from your skincare regimen. You want to reverse your skin's aging and lock it into a youthful state for life, but most individuals fall way short of this goal. The missing second piece is to invest in and use what works, and then toss what doesn't. This is much easier said than accomplished, however. It is estimated that roughly only 20 percent of available skincare creams and serums have any substantial anti-aging qualities to them.

Why is something so simple so difficult to do? There are a multitude of reasons:

1. MARKETING MYTHS AND GIMMICKS.

We are conditioned into believing that a rare plant essence equates with efficacy, or that going 100 percent organic in our skincare indicates that the pureness of the lotion or serum will make our skin young—or at least prevent aging. Unequivocally, these products feel and smell luxurious, are probably good for the environment, and are fun to use, but they do not necessarily have significant anti-aging powers.

2. EMPTY STUDIES.

Anytime you read the words, "Blank percent of users experienced, felt, or saw improvement in," it signifies that the study was a poor one at best. Keep in mind that the study participants could have massaged Vaseline™ into their facial skin with some superficial improvement in their complexions, softness, and appearance. The bare minimum that a good study needs is at least a placebo cream as well as sensitive instruments that quantify the results along with what anti-aging properties it intends to deliver. And lastly, the active ingredient needs to deliver results that achieve statistical significance. To a large cosmetic corporation, it always sounds better to run an ad that states, "98 percent of women expe-

rienced...," or, "86 percent would recommend it to a friend," rather than there was a 12 percent reduction in wrinkle depth or 8 percent increase in firmness. Low numbers just don't help sales.

3. BOOKS WRITTEN BY EXPERTS WITH SECONDARY MOTIVES TO PROMOTE THEIR OWN PRODUCTS.

There are many skincare books on the bookstore shelves written by some of the top specialists in the industry. They are without a doubt full of current research findings and have provided you, the consumer, with knowledge to think past the marketing gimmicks of the large cosmetic companies. Unfortunately, most of the books promote *only* the products and active ingredients that the experts intend to themselves sell. Keep in mind that book publishing is the method many specialists use to launch their product lines to the public. You may not be getting the full picture, and it may be skewed.

4. BUSY PRACTICES.

What about skincare advice from your dermatologist, plastic surgeon, or esthetician working in the emerging medical spas and offices? Keep in mind that physicians have a universe of knowledge to acquire to make it to their levels of expertise. This

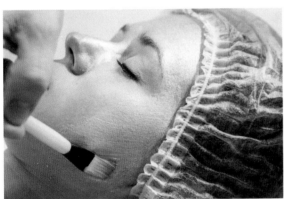

knowledge might include surgeries, cancers, diseases, allergies, autoimmune disorders, to name a few. Many medical specialists are simply too busy to find the time to do the research and keep up with the reading on all the emerging and current anti-aging research. When they do recommend products, it is sometimes influenced by the cosmeceutical representatives that service the office. This means that doctors and staff often depend on the these representatives to supply them with the necessary information to promote their product lines. Naturally, any representative with a monthly sales quota hanging over their heads will sell the physicians and staff on why their products are better than the competition.

5. THE WHAT'S ON THE SHELF APPROACH THAT MAY OR MAY NOT DELIVER

Estheticians are also limited to promoting what happens to be on the shelf at the spa they're working at. Even during the training period, they usually only learn about the skincare the academy promotes. In the real world of esthetician training, they spend hours learning facial massage techniques, waxing, extractions, and sanitization, etc. The exam they need to pass to get their license is stringent and focuses a lot on sanitization as the public's health and welfare is at stake. But that leaves just six to nine

months of training, with little time to go into great depth of the aging process. There are terrific estheticians out there, but more often then not, the best ones are those who spend a lot of their own time researching anti-aging techniques and products.

This book has been created to be the unbiased missing link between the current findings in the medical literature and you the consumer. It is the culmination of years of careful research into most, if not all, the respectable studies looking into what if any efficacy—and exactly how much efficacy—various cosmetic actives can deliver. It gives you, the consumer, a bird's-eye-view into the efficacy hierarchy of various topical anti-aging treatments so that you can make better decisions about the anti-agers you purchase. It allows you to use what works, and toss those that don't.

THE MOST-POWERFUL COMBINATION

THE THIRD MISSING LINK of the break-the-age-code puzzle is to understand the difference between a skin strengthener and a skin stimulator. Without question, efficacy is of critical importance in any serum or cream you spend your hard-earned cash on.

However, understanding how that topical works inside your skin is just as critical to keeping your skin young for life. Ask yourself, "How is this treatment working on my skin?" Many of us cannot answer that question, or we may come up with an answer the salesperson told us such as "it's nourishing," or "it wakes up my skin cells," or "it's revitalizing." You don't see a measurable difference in wrinkle reduction and firmness, but your skin does seem soft and revitalized. What's happening inside your skin?

In reality, most of the botanicals and vitamins act as antioxidants or anti-inflammatories, and are nourishing because they prevent or at least slow down the harm to your skin. Most nourishers are preventers, or as others refer to it, strengtheners. They guard against the free-radical havoc and inflammation. Others guard against deadly enzymes called matrix metalloproteinases (MMP inhibitors) or advanced glycation end products. The guardian effect on skin cells and collagen matrix is of particular importance to post-menopausal women who need more than ever to protect what they have as their bodies are less able to manufacture more of the youthful components that make up younger skin.

Most of us are now buying a lot of these products,

including that rare melon extract, grape seed extract, resveratrol, most forms of vitamin C, and plant stem cells to name just a few. Some work inside skin cells to quench the free-radical destruction and inflammatory cascade, while others work outside skin cells. These would be your anti-glycation or enzyme-inhibiting compounds that directly protect the collagen network. Some researchers have called these compounds skin strengtheners because the skin cells don't need to use up critical energy to prevent and repair the daily assault as they become stronger—skin appears more vibrant. It takes less effort for the skin to maintain its own equilibrium. It slows the trajectory into old-aged skin, but sadly skin will still succumb into a downward path trajectory, just more slowly.

THAT'S WHERE STIMULATORS FIT IN as the third critical tier of Young Skin for Life. Stimulators are compounds that trigger your skin to do something it normally wouldn't do. In other words, they work in a totally different fashion than strengtheners do. They stimulate cells to do extraordinary things. Some are very powerful and lock directly into skin cell receptors—triggering a whole host of events to happen in your skin, from producing more collagen, elastin, moisture cells, and blood vessels, to affect-

ing DNA transcription. Some examples of receptor-site activity are vitamin D, estrogen, retinoic acid (Retin A), and even certain forms of vitamin B.

Remember: many parts of your body contain cells with receptor sites. When substances such as hormones and other molecules uniquely fit into these receptor sites, powerful effects ensue. That's why drug companies develop molecules that are able to fit into distinct receptor sites to produce disease-altering changes in the body. They are highly effective, and skin actives that use similar receptor power can hugely alter the aging process inside your skin.

But not all skin stimulators harness the power of skin cell receptors. Other skin stimulators include peptides, growth factors, and elastin agonists. High doses of a certain formulation of vitamin C can also have a triggering effect on skin. It can create a more youthful and vibrant-looking skin if used consistently by permanently locking your skin into a youth mode and keeping it there. Of course, not all stimulators work the same way, are equally as potent, or are for everyone. And while they are not quick fixes, if used with skin smoothing and strengthening, they can powerfully lock your skin into a visibly much more youthful appearance—wrinkle free and even-toned.

MANY ANTI-AGING SERUMS AND LOTIONS CONTAIN A COCKTAIL OF STRENGTHEN-ERS AND STIMULATORS.

Sadly, however, most skin stimulators available today are extremely low on the efficacy scale and will have modest results at best. Along with avoiding skin smoothing, it probably is the biggest reason women are always ultimately disappointed in their current treatment.

What to watch out for? An example of a weak skincare ingredient is retinyl palmitate found in a staggering amount of anti-aging creams, serums, and lotions. You are told that it is the strongest wrinkle-reducing ingredient available, but in reality, it has to undergo a very lengthy metabolic conversion process (see Skin Pearls Retinoids) to have any beneficial stimulating effects in skin. Experts estimate that the stimulating effects are only about one-twentieth the strength of a prescription retinoid. Don't let any marketer or skin expert try to convince you that these substances work the same as the prescription products, just more slowly and without the side effects. There is no scientific data to support this claim.

ANOTHER WEAK STIMULATOR IS A CLASS OF PEPTIDES THAT ACT ON NEUROTRANS-MITTERS

By increasing them while providing a modest tightening of skin, or slowing them down in an effort to relax wrinkles. Their effects are minimal, and they do nothing to build the skin's youthful structure back to what it once was in its more youthful days.

The current commercial showing discarded, half-empty jars of skin cream, referred to as a graveyard, speaks to a lot of women. The jars are half empty and thrown out because they were ultimately considered to be a waste of money. These jars of cream may have created a degree of vibrancy, but they didn't significantly turn back the clock on the skin's appearance. Skin was not more wrinkle free, smoother, or firmer. Women are seeking a quick fix, and they come to the conclusion that if they don't experience immediate results, the product is ineffective. Or at least that's what the commercial and others like them want you to believe.

WHEN EQUATING SPEED WITH EFFICACY IS NOT A GOOD IDEA

Over time, with those thoughts in the back of their minds, women begin to equate efficacy with how fast a skin cream or serum works. As a result, they turn to superficial effects of products that can temporarily plump dead cells and give a smoother appearance, or others that tweak skin lipids surrounding the dead cells and temporarily tighten skin. When they choose these types of products over effective strengtheners and stimulators, they miss the opportunity to truly help their skin become younger from the ground up. In other words, their skin is still on a downward-sliding trajectory. Instead of quick, superficial fixes, women should insist on using stimulators and strengtheners that are effective. You'll find their efficacy status presented in a birds-eye view on the pages that follow.

BY USING THE RIGHT INGREDIENTS, AND
THE METHOD I PRESENT IN THIS BOOK,
YOU CAN BRING YOUR SKIN BACK IN TIME
AND LOCK IT INTO YOUTH MODE FOR LIFE.

THE SYSTEM: SMOOTH • STRENGTHEN • STIM-
ULATE is highly effective because it is based on
scientific facts and not marketing fluff. It has worked
for me and for many of my previous clients. Although
your skin will appear more vibrant in a matter of
days, it takes weeks to repair and strengthen your
dermal repair zone or safety net. But those weeks
matter. Weeks add up to months, months add up
to years, and years add up to a lifetime. Enjoying
young skin for life is within all of our reach.

THE SYSTEM

SMOOTH | STRENGTHEN | STIMULATE

Chapter 6

THE SYSTEM
SMOOTH
STRENGTHEN
STIMULATE

YOUR CHOICE OF PRODUCTS
IS CRITICAL TO KEEPING YOUR
SKIN YOUNG AND WRINKLE FREE.
ENSURE YOUR SKINCARE IS
INCLUDING AT LEAST ONE ACTIVE
FROM EACH CATEGORY – SMOOTH,
STRENGTHEN, STIMULATE.

THE **SYSTEM**

SMOOTH STRENGTHEN STIMULATE

A funny thing happened while on my honeymoon a year ago—I forgot to pack my smoother. If you have come this far in your reading, you know that by smoother I mean exfoliator. And you already know the benefits of an exfoliator are almost too many to list. But here are the top 3:

• Diminishes the corneocyte plugs that "wedge" in wrinkles

• Sends signals to your dermis below to start producing more collagen

• Allows for much better penetration of your anti-aging treatments

At the time, I was using dry-cleansing grains that I could incorporate with my cleanser. By doing so, I could tailor the amount of exfoliation my skin could handle. This was important because I find that while traveling, my skin can become easily sensitized by changing environments and air travel.

However, when you travel, you'll often have to compromise and make do with whatever culture you happen to be in. In other words, I didn't expect to find the cleansing grains I was looking for. However, I told myself that any form of an effective exfoliator would do—I wasn't going to be fussy. I just didn't want my skin to start developing wrinkles as an unwanted souvenir of the trip. Two weeks without exfoliating my skin would without a doubt start encouraging wrinkles.

To make a long story short, my husband and I went on a daylong quest for anything that would fit the bill. Alpha hydroxy acids, cleansing grains, exfoliating pads, sponges—we looked everywhere but to no avail. We finally stumbled on a savvy salesperson who directed us to a specialty pharmacy in town that carried, as he put it, "unusual" products. We somehow managed to find the specialty pharmacy, which was filled with physician-formulated products. We found only two products that would work as effective smoothers. We were relieved, however, that we could enjoy our trip without worrying that our skin would be deprived of this vital step.

During our stay in the beautiful European nation, I could not help but notice the huge discrepancy in appearance between the young and the old. Wom-

en's skin in this country did not age well. In older women, skin tones were sadly extremely wrinkled. Sadder still, their skin wrinkled at a relatively young age. I knew in my heart—and after reviewing numerous research studies—that they didn't have to age in this ungraceful manner. Their nation is known for its luscious fragrances, and fashion but the skincare frankly wasn't doing the women there any favors. I am convinced that part of the reason for this was that they had bought into the notion that exfoliation was not a daily necessity. After looking high and low, and not finding a proper skin smoother, I confidently believe their notion not to exfoliate daily plays a tremendous role in the premature deterioration of their skin. Yes, genetics, sun, and smoking also play a role, but I believe to this day that the women were missing out on this vital step.

Please try to incorporate this smoothing step in your daily toilette, as the French call it. I recommend adding exfoliating grains to your cleanser so that you and you alone are in control of the intensity of your skin smoothing. I have also seen superior results when clients have switched from chemical exfoliants to physical exfoliants. Remember that chemical smoothers loosen the cement that holds the outer dead cells together, and they may not provide the

amount of skin smoothing you need to discourage wrinkle formation. They are also tricky to use as their strength depends upon the pH value.

Your SMOOTH mantra? "Start low and go slow." Don't push the amount of buffing beads up too soon. Let your skin adjust and make sure to use circular movements with your fingertips. Your skin and your appearance will thank you for it. And don't be surprised if you receive compliments after the very first week!

Please refer to your Skin Pearls Glossary for more information about the benefits and risks associated with chemical or physical smoothers.

THE **SYSTEM**

PROTECT YOUR YOUTH

Anytime you see the words, nourish, revitalize, awaken you're probably getting what I call skin strengthener. These consist of anti-inflammatories, antioxidants and other compounds that "protect" your collagen.
I call these "collagen keepers."

Why do you need strengtheners? Because a lot of small things add up to bigger things, much bigger. All the little "hits" the free radical marauder "drive bys" inflict on your skin cells can eventually lead all the way to your skin cells DNA and you don't want that to happen.

WHAT STRENGTHENERS DO:

1. Stop the free-radical destruction you get from UV rays to pollution and other toxins.

2. Stop the inflammatory cascade that results if the free radicals gang up and create bigger damage.

3. Allow your cells to keep themselves energized by guarding the mitochondria. Your skin cells can respond better to other actives that stimulate repair.

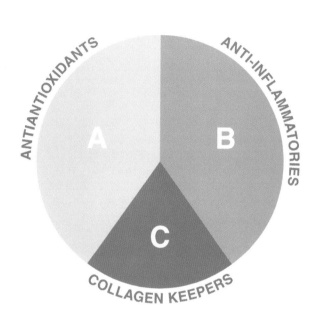

Don't let your skin be without it's A,B,C's.

BEATINFLAMMATION

Chronic Inflammation

Destructive chronic inflammation can be prevented and reversed by the consumption of proper food, oral supplements, and other targeted ingredients. Preventing and reversing chronic inflammation not only helps to prevent aging, it also prevents many other skin conditions and diseases. This is particularly important if you live, work, or play in a high-stress or harsh environment. Environmental insults such as cigarette smoke, pollution, harsh skincare regimens, preservatives, and other irritants can disrupt your stratum corneum, or skin barrier, and activate the release of molecules that trigger an inflammatory cascade. Look at the ingredients in your moisturizer—choose a moisturizer rich in ceramides that help boost skin's natural barrier and seal in moisture. Shea butter, olive oil, and almond oil are also effective. The moisturizer, along with your anti-inflammatory ingredients, will work synergistically to restore the normal function to your skin.

Go From Good to Great

What makes a good anti-inflammatory a great one? When it is so powerful that it can halt the destructive inflammatory cascade from the number-one skin ager—the sun. The evidence is overwhelming that green tea is an all-star because it can help protect skin from skin cancer after exposure to UV light. In fact, one recent study showed that applying green tea directly to skin 30 minutes before UV exposure significantly reduced resulting sunburn and DNA damage. Remember—the more your DNA is damaged, the less able your skin is to repair itself like it did in its youth, and the faster you will age.

A DAILY BEAUTY-PROOF UPGRADE

Even if you are not using a moisturizer or sunscreen that contains green tea, you can still reap the beauty-proof benefits it delivers by enjoying at least two cups of green tea throughout the day. This is important, particularly if you tend to skimp on SPF. Drinking green tea can still protect your skin from sunburn and skin cancer after exposure to UV light, and it has other major benefits as follows:

• The beauty benefits of green tea accrue over time. In one study over a six-month period of time, participants who drank two to three cups of green tea a day showed significant improvement in sun damage. Roughness, overall redness, and even broken capillaries were greatly improved. It has also been shown to help prevent blood sugar spikes.

• Remember the glycation chapter? This chapter explains how sugars and starches age your skin by attaching to collagen, stiffening and damaging your youth network. When you enjoy a cup of green tea as a part of your daily beauty habit, you're also helping your skin thwart the glycated end products that yellow your skin and age you almost as fast as the sun does. So skimp on some of those lattes and sodas, and consider adding a high-quality green tea in their place. There are many good varieties to choose from. A personal favorite that I discovered on a recent trip to France is Mariage Frères tea. This company has recently gone international and it creates some of the most-delicious teas on the market today.

Just as you should eliminate tap water from your diet whenever possible, brew your tea with your favorite bottled spring water, or at the very least, filtered water. Tap water contains chlorine that can react with organic materials to make very unfriendly, skin DNA-altering substances. What's more, the improvement in taste is undeniable. What is my favorite water? Evian. There is a reason almost every restaurant in Paris has it on the menu—it simply tastes the best. You're worth it!

One last question you may have: Why green tea? Green tea has been used as a medicine for thousands of years throughout Asia because of its many benefits—from lowering blood pressure to preventing cancer. The reason green tea has more health benefits than black tea is due to its processing. Black tea is processed in a way that allows fermentation, whereas green tea's processing prevents fermentation from occurring. The end result is that green tea retains the maximum amounts of polyphenols and antioxidants.

USE ACTIVES - SUCH AS GREEN TEA - ON THE HIGH END OF THE SCALE FOR MAXIMUM ANTI-INFLAMMATORY BENEFITS.

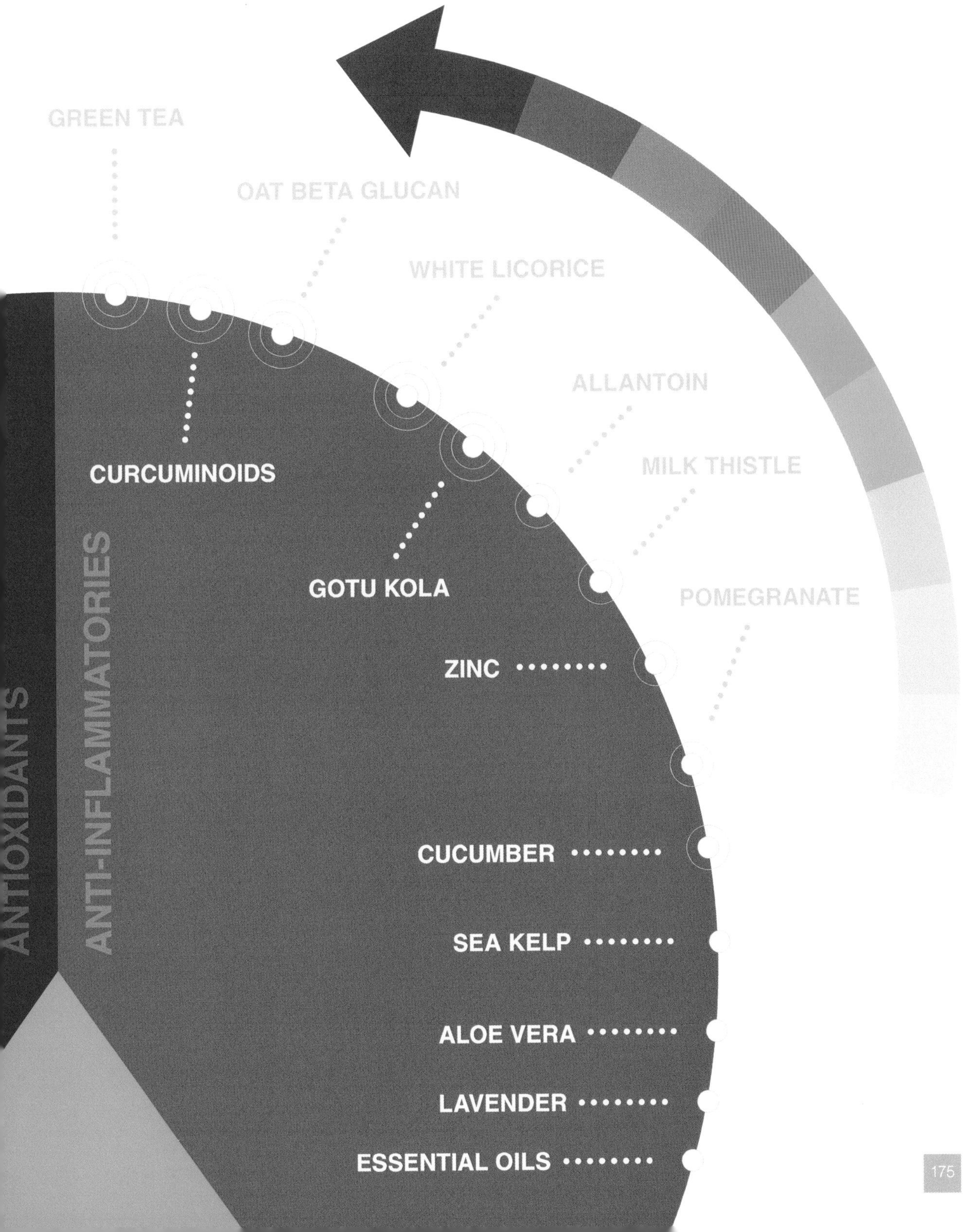

GREEN TEA

OAT BETA GLUCAN

WHITE LICORICE

ALLANTOIN

MILK THISTLE

ANTIOXIDANTS

ANTI-INFLAMMATORIES

CURCUMINOIDS

GOTU KOLA

POMEGRANATE

ZINC

CUCUMBER

SEA KELP

ALOE VERA

LAVENDER

ESSENTIAL OILS

THE SYSTEM

SMOOTH **STRENGTHEN** STIMULATE

We've all heard the fashion expression that less is more, but in the case of antioxidants, more really is more. Please do not rely on only one antioxidant for your anti-aging regimen. As you learned in reading this book, each antioxidant likes to work a little differently than the rest. Many like to linger in different parts of your skin cells. Some prefer the watery parts, others the lipid areas. If you use several antioxidants, you are much more likely to ensure that each and every area of your skin cells is protected.

New research into the proven benefits of antioxidants to protect your skin cells keeps pouring in every day. Many (see Skin Pearls Glossary) have been found to provide additional protection against the number-one free-radical generator—the sun. Many antioxidants also are effective at quelling inflammation, a big skin ager. Picking a few antioxidants from the chart will ensure your skin receives a hefty dose of anti-aging benefits.

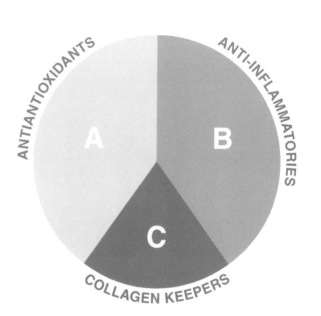

"When you were young your skin had high levels of built-in antioxidants. As you age your levels diminish. Break the skin aging by incorporating an army of potent antioxidants into your skincare regimen."

VITAMIN C+E+F

IDEBENONE

COQ10

MARINE ALGAE

RESVERATROL

ALPHA LIPOIC ACID

ASTAXANTHIN

VITAMIN E

ACAI BERRY

SILYMARIN

•••••••• LYCOPENE

•••••••• GRAPE SEED

•••••••• COCOA SEED

•••••••• PLANT STEM CELLS

•••••••• COFFEE BERRY

ANTIOXIDANTS

ANTI-INFLAMMATORIES

THE SYSTEM

SMOOTH STRENGTHEN STIMULATE

STIMULATORS

Stimulators are agents that go beyond protection. They stimulate your skin cells to do things they normally wouldn't do, such as switching to a robust repair mode. Stimulators accomplish this by triggering your collagen and elastin factories to go into high gear. This creates a newer and better dermal network that repairs wrinkles and inhibits new ones from forming. And that's just the beginning. Even the most-potent antioxidants, anti-inflammatories, or other strengtheners are not going to give your skin the youthifying benefits a good stimulator will. Please don't neglect this vital step. A good stimulator can visibly transform your skin. Refer to your Skin Pearls Glossary to learn more.

CONSULT WITH A SPECIALIST IN THE FIELD OF ANTI-AGING MEDICINE.

5

HORMONES

4

YOUR SKIN HAS OVER 150 GROWTH FACTORS THAT DIMINISH AS YOU AGE. LOOK FOR PRODUCTS WITH MULTIPLE GROWTH FACTORS AND CYTOKINES.

GROWTH FACTORS

STIMULATE

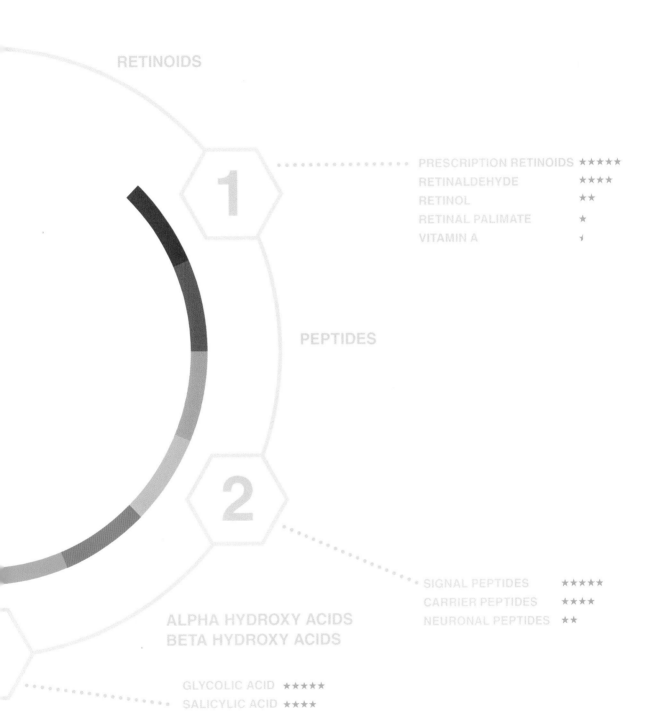

RETINOIDS

PRESCRIPTION RETINOIDS ★★★★★
RETINALDEHYDE ★★★★
RETINOL ★★
RETINAL PALIMATE ★
VITAMIN A ⌐

PEPTIDES

SIGNAL PEPTIDES ★★★★★
CARRIER PEPTIDES ★★★★
NEURONAL PEPTIDES ★★

ALPHA HYDROXY ACIDS
BETA HYDROXY ACIDS

GLYCOLIC ACID ★★★★★
SALICYLIC ACID ★★★★
LACTIC ACID ★★★

STIMULATE

Chapter 7

YOUR INSTANT ANTI-AGING DIET UPGRADE

181

07

AN INSTANT UPGRADE TO YOUR ANTI-AGING DIET

Using THE SYSTEM will help diminish the signs of wrinkles you already have and lock your skin into a youth mode for life. By upgrading your skincare with products that contain more-powerful ingredients, and incorporating the skin-smoothing techniques within this book, you will reap the most-superior, scientifically proven anti-aging benefits available anywhere to date.

DIETARY CHANGES

Throughout this book you've discovered dietary age breakers that can reduce inflammation and toxic overload and suppress the ravaging effects of glycated end products. You've read about improving your ratio of omega oils, cutting down on white bread, sugars, and anything that contains high-fructose corn syrup. And you've read about including network antioxidants in your supplements like vitamin C, E, alpha lipoic acid, and CoQ10. It is also critically important that you address your hormones with a physician knowledgeable in the field of hormone replacement.

However, there's a missing piece of the aging puzzle that is something most likely lacking in everyone's diet. That missing link is protein. More specifically, it is very important to include small, consistent portions of protein throughout your day.

RETHINK PROTEIN—TIMING IS CRITICAL

New research points to a missing link that can help keep your skin youthful. You can eat all the fresh, organic, antioxidant-rich fruits and vegetables in the world, but if you don't supply your skin with the building blocks it needs from protein, it will age prematurely. And, as you will see, it's not only the amounts of protein that are critical to keeping young skin, but the timing is just as important, if not more so.

The reason most of us haven't given much thought to consistently fueling our skin by eating protein every few hours is because, until now, there hasn't been any research to prove its benefits. Who would have thought that timing could be so critical? A new study published in *Nutrition and Metabolism* took a closer look at how the timing of protein intake, perhaps more so than the amount, has a major impact on how well our body's strength and structure is maintained. The researchers concluded that consuming protein every three hours or so is vitally important to muscle-protein synthesis. This dietary change produced significantly more muscle growth—around 25 percent—compared to those who consumed their protein mostly at dinner. And when we really think about it, the average American diet looks something like this: A carbohydrate-heavy breakfast, a sandwich or salad for lunch, and usual-

ly an overly large serving of protein for dinner. That falls far short from maintaining a consistent intake of protein over the course of the day that our body and skin needs to thrive.

Lets take another look at some of the reasons we eat this way, and at the American diet in general. Today, some experts feel that the American food pyramid created in 1991, may have helped create the obesity and diabetic epidemic currently on the rise in the United States. As you'll see, this food pyramid has not only been harmful to our health, but it has also been harmful to our skin. If you find that hard to believe, consider this fact: The number of overweight Americans has risen 61 percent since the pyramid was introduced. The pyramid suggests that the majority of food we eat each day—6 to 11 servings—come from the grains and carbohydrate groups. The pyramid narrows as you move upward—to fewer servings of fruits and vegetables, and still fewer protein-rich foods. It is ultimately capped off with fats and oils, which we are told to use sparingly.

When the updated pyramid was created, it almost instantaneously appeared on the sides of pasta boxes, bread wrappers, and packages of other foods that resided in the grains and carbohydrate category. The thinking at the time was that if we could all lower our fat intake, we would consume fewer calories and fewer Americans would be obese. But this low-fat dieting strategy backfired and made us fat. This is because the pyramid recommenda-

tions opened the floodgates by giving us permission to consume huge portions of fat-free snacks and meals—all packed with sugar, flour, and other carbohydrates. Not only are the fat-free, carbohydrate-rich meals and snacks full of calories, we eat more because without enough fat and protein, our hunger is never satiated and we are always looking forward to the next snack or meal.

When it comes to diabetes, the grains and carbohydrate groupings that comprise the largest base of the pyramid will ultimately become sugar in the bloodstream that helps trigger development of the disease. Another consequence of consuming a carbohydrate-rich diet is the creation of aging-related developments in your skin such as yellowing, wrinkles, and coarseness. Remember the chapter on glycation? I discussed the aging that happens in your skin when sugars, by way of a non-enzymatic process, attach to collagen—stiffening, and breaking the fibers in the same way that sugars stick to blood vessel walls of patients with diabetes.

The national food pyramid is now in question because of the increase in the prevalence of obesity and diabetes in the United States. It is certain that the food pyramid will be modified once again to include more healthy oils and proteins in the future. For basic health reasons, along with a serious

anti-aging skin strategy, you may want to modify the amounts of carbohydrates, proteins, and oils you eat.

Regardless of a possible future change to the food pyramid, the current pyramid image is stuck inside our minds. As a result, it's not just okay to consume a tremendous amount of carbohydrates; we believe it's good for us because the government tells us it is. It's no wonder we save most of our protein intake for dinner and that carbohydrates have become a priority in our food pyramid mindset.

AMOUNTS ARE ALSO CRITICAL

The initial study I referenced in this chapter shows us that protein needs to be consistently available for our bodies to function best, and that goes for our skin too. The amount of protein you consume is also important, and experts state that women's protein intake is often lacking. This is often attributed to our obsession with dieting and our fast-paced lifestyles that leave little room during a hectic day for healthy eating.

Protein intake has been studied extensively for its anti-aging skin benefits. Scientists have studied what happens to skin when protein is restricted as well as what happens inside skin when protein is increased. Let's first consider what happens when your skin becomes deprived of protein. In this case, not only was total collagen content reduced, but the quality of collagen declined significantly as well.

So, what does the quality of collagen have to do with young skin?

There are several types of collagen in our skin and they change over time. In young skin, collagen type I accounts for about 80 percent, and type III about 15 percent. Interestingly enough, a baby's skin does not scar. Collagen type I is thought to play a role in this phenomenon. The ratio of type III to type I increases with age, meaning that as we age, we produce less type I and more type III. A diet deprived of protein triggers skin to prematurely produce aging-associated type III collagen. Another study from the *Journal of Physiology* found that the total amount of collagen in our bodies is diminished by a lack of protein. When investigators delved further, they discovered that most of the collagen loss occurred in skin and not in other parts of our bodies. They also discovered that protein deficiency not only affects collagen, but also has a profound affect on diminishing moisture-binding cells of the dermis called glycosaminoglycans, or GAGS.

A trend emerging around the world is the inclusion of a type of protein in the form of collagen—specifically collagen from animal sources that has been hydrolyzed into an absorbable form. Hydrolyzed collagen supplements are huge in Asia and just beginning to take off in the U.S. market. A 2011 study found that collagen supplements, or protein, not only increased collagen levels as expected, but also suppressed an enzyme you have read about in this book. This type of enzyme falls in the family known

as metalloproteinases, or MMP's. The supplements worked both on increasing what our skin needs most while slowing down the forces that destroy it—remember that our skin is 75 percent collagen. The authors concluded that this type of protein supplementation might be helpful in reducing age-related changes in the dermis.

There are many skeptics when it comes to collagen supplements, but the efficacy evidence is slowly emerging. The most recent, well-designed, double-blinded, placebo-controlled study published in *Skin Pharmacology and Physiology* 2014 found that the primary endpoint, skin elasticity, was significantly improved in women who took 2.5 to 5 grams of hydrolyzed collagen once daily for 8 weeks. With the evidence mounting about protein, timing, and hydrolyzed collagen supplements, you really need to rethink the timing and amounts of protein you consume. It would be judicious to include small portions of protein throughout your day along with collagen supplementation twice daily. Make sure that your protein is what is called complete which includes all the amino acids your skin needs. Complete protein comes from animal, fish, soy, whey, and dairy sources. I like to make smoothies from Greek yogurt or whey mixed with low-sugar pomegranate or acai juice. That way I don't drive up the calories and sugars, and I am consuming complete proteins found in yogurt and whey. It's fast and easy and I not only feel better and am less hungry, but also have more energy. I like knowing that I'm giving my skin the fuel it needs to stay young and you will too.

Five serious anti-aging dietary enrichments

1. TIMING IS VITAL

Enjoy small portions of protein throughout the day. Please don't make the mistake of investing in protein bars before you check the labeling because many contain high-fructose corn syrup in addition to unhealthy preservatives. Low-sugar juices such as pomegranate or acai juice mixed with low-fat Greek yogurt or whey protein or soymilk is an excellent choice and an easy way to eat smaller portions without the calories. In addition, protein gummy snacks are now available in most pharmacies. Consider adding hydrolyzed collagen supplements to the mix twice daily. Data on the supplement BioSil also looks promising for its anti-aging benefits.

Remember the golden rule: Protein is the building block of all skin cells. We can include all the healthy fruits and vegetables in the world that protect our skin cells and help drive down inflammation, but skin needs the fuel from protein to repair and renew itself. Your skin is not only replacing the cells in the upper layer—the epidermis—every 28 days, it is also constantly producing collagen, elastin, and GAGs that keep your skin firm and smooth. These are the reasons why protein is so critical.

2. NETWORK POWER

Make sure your diet or supplements include the five powerful all-stars. Eating a variety of fruits and vegetables is one way to get diverse antioxidants,

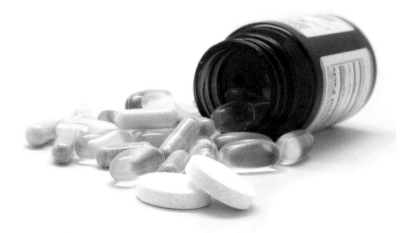

but research has shown that five antioxidants—only five out of thousands—stand out as superior to others. These antioxidants work best as a team. Each serves a different skin cell protective function and enhances the activity of each other. In other words, they work stronger and for a longer amount of time when combined, which is what you want for your skin because most antioxidants have a much shorter lifespan.

The anti-aging all-stars are vitamin C, E, alpha lipoic acid, CoQ10, and glutathione. Glutathione is perhaps the biggest defender out of all five all-stars against free radicals, but the levels in our skin begin to decline in our 40s. Unfortunately, our bodies cannot absorb it in pill form because the molecules are too large; therefore, we have to primarily manufacture it ourselves. But, you can help your body manufacture it by supplementing with alpha lipoic acid and eating foods such as walnuts, avocados, cauliflower, broccoli, and tomatoes. Some other foods that have been shown to stimulate the production of glutathione are Brussels sprouts, cabbage, spinach, and watermelon.

Alpha lipoic acid not only protects your skin cells, but because it is both water and fat soluble, it also helps protect your skin against the ravaging effects of any sugars you might consume. Some foods such as kidney, liver, spinach, and broccoli contain alpha lipoic acid, but in extremely small amounts. Even if you don't like supplements, you probably should invest in alpha lipoic acid to ensure you're getting enough.

Vitamin C has almost too many skin benefits to mention. It is the only vitamin, when used topically in the right concentration and formulation (see Skin Pearls) that can actually stimulate collagen synthesis. However, even if you do use it topically, make sure your diet contains vitamin-rich foods found in most fruits and vegetables.

Vitamins E and C help protect skin from UV radiation. After a week of Vitamin E supplements, our skin oils pick it up and deliver its UV protection benefits. I recommend the following:

• Alpha lipoic acid, 50 mg twice daily

• CoQ10, 50 mg twice daily

• Vitamin C, 500 to 1,500 mg daily

• Vitamin E, 400 to 800 IU daily

3. BREAK THE BONDS

Cut back on white bread, sugars, and especially foods containing high-fructose corn syrup—sodas, ice cream bars, and most snacks. Studies have found that cutting back on high-fructose corn syrup helps halt the increase of glycated end products responsible for collagen stiffening and breakage that ultimately spell wrinkles and slack skin. It has also been linked to the general yellowing of the skin's complexion. You will see a new skin clarity and suppleness if you refrain from anything that spikes the glucose levels in your bloodstream. Consuming small portions of protein throughout the day will also ward off the high spikes in blood sugars that wreak havoc in your skin.

4. SWITCH OILS

Consider supplements such as fish or flax seed oil, or at the very least, switch the oils in your kitchen cupboard to olive oil. This improves your good -to-bad oil ratio that has major anti-inflammatory benefits to your entire body as well as your skin. The health benefits from such a simple thing as switching oils and improving your omega ratio is staggering.

5. SUPER SKIN FOODS

• **SOY.** Soy, tofu, and other soy foods may help to preserve skin-firming collagen because they are rich in isoflavones. Testing results using mice indicated that consuming soy products provides protection from UV-induced wrinkle formation. A study published in the *Journal of the American College of Nutrition* demonstrated that mice fed isoflavones had fewer wrinkles and smoother skin than mice that were exposed to UV light but didn't get isoflavones.

• **STRAWBERRIES.** Just one cup of strawberries delivers a whopping 150 percent of your daily requirement for vitamin C. According to reasearch from the *Journal of Clinical Nutrition* in 2007, vitamin C-rich foods may help ward off wrinkles and age-related dryness.

• **TOMATOES.** They contain an abundant amount of lycopene, a nutrient that has many proven skin benefits—one of which is smoother skin. A study published in 2008 in the *European Journal of Pharmaceutics and Biopharmaceutics* found that in the 20 individuals studied, those who had higher concentrations of lycopene in their system had smoother skin. Another benefit of lycopene is the protection it provides from skin-damaging UV rays. In one study, participants who ate just 2½ tablespoons of tomato paste over a period of several weeks had 50 percent less reddening after sun exposure. Research has shown that when lycopene levels were increased by way of supplements, there was no significant UV protection, but you can increase your levels of lycopene with significant UV protection by consuming power foods like tomatoes or carrot juice.

• **TEA, RED WINE, COCOA.** All three contain a type of flavonoid called epicatechin. In a study of 24 women published in the *Journal of Nutrition*, drinking a cocoa beverage over a period of 12 weeks improved skin texture. Epicatechin increases blood flow to the skin, boosting oxygen and nutrient supply.

• **SALMON, SARDINES, TUNA.** These fish are a rich source for omega-3s. Eicosapentaenoic acid, or EPA, is one of the omega-3s that has been shown to preserve collagen fibers that help keep skin firm. Eating salmon, in particular, has been shown to significantly drive down inflammation levels in skin.

• **ACAI.** Acai berries have been shown to have up to 33 times more antioxidant power than red wine or grapes. It boasts a range of unique plant chemical compounds that are not found in any other fruit. One of those compounds, called anthocyanin, has been shown to be one of the most-potent antioxidants to date, protecting skin's collagen, helping maintain a healthy vascular network, and driving down inflammation. Acai's oxygen radical absorbance capacity, or ORAC level, is over 3,500, which is hundreds of times higher than your average fruits like apples and bananas.

• **WALNUTS.** Walnuts are full of omega–3 fatty acids that improve elasticity. They also contain copper, a mineral that can help boost collagen production. Researchers have been known to call the free-radical scavenging power of antioxidants found in walnuts remarkable. When tested for levels of skin-benefiting polyphenols, walnuts were among the highest.

• **CHIA.** Chia has a higher percentage of protein than any other grain. It also is a complete protein our skin requires to thrive. It is high in fiber and can help regulate blood sugar levels and sweep debris out of your intestines to help detoxify your system naturally. Chia has higher antioxidant levels than blueberries and has a shelf life of 4 to 5 years. Chia has the highest known percentage of linoleic fatty acid— more than flax seed and salmon.

Chapter 8

THE FUTURE
OF SKINCARE

08

THE FUTURE IS FORWARD

We've come a long way from the era when cleanse, tone, and moisturize was the accepted norm. We all believed this because the cosmetic companies espoused that this method was the key—the magic formula for younger-looking skin. Unfortunately, today's science proves that this worn-out cosmetic industry mantra is wrong. Scientists and many skin specialists have accepted the fact that moisturizing alone is not enough to control skin aging. The filling of outer dead cells with water, much like pouring water on a sponge, is not going to affect the aging process in any way, shape, or form. Skin is now being viewed as the living, functioning organ it truly is. Just like all our organs and bodily tissues, it needs nutrients to survive, thrive, and remain youthful. A new era has arrived where the future of anti-aging is focused on impacting living skin cells with nutrients and stimulating actives. In other words, we are more and more focused on the living cells themselves, not the vast landscape of our outer surface of dead skin cells and hardened lipids. That's just a start—science is delving even deeper.

Next-generation anti-aging labs are springing up all around the world. They are often working hand-in-hand with medical departments focusing on genetics and genomic sciences. Together, they study how actives influence everything from aging to sun damage on a genetic level. They will track how actives in serums and moisturizers influence changes in collagen and elastin production, inflammation, pigmentation, and influence cellular repair by way of the DNA itself. In other words, we are telescoping deeper into what we all want to control—our skin's aging process.

Here is just one example of what is taking place in our own country. American scientific ingenuity has narrowed down on the key genes that affect skin and the aging process. We have approximately 20,000 genes in the body—148 of those are now classified as the skin's anti-aging genes. Science is on the verge of learning key ways to influence those genes and, hence, influence our skin's aging process. The future is exciting indeed!

And where will the future cell and DNA-altering actives come from? Many believe that the sea itself holds the answers. Microalgae is becoming an increasingly popular all-star. It grows in an amazing mineral medium that terrestrial plants lack, and absorbs high concentrations of a variety of different nutrients beneficial to skin. Depending on the environment in which the algae grows, it will develop cell functions as defense mechanisms to protect itself from various aggressors. Because of this, algae and other marine life have been found to contain amazing peptides, antioxidants, and enzymes that can effectively alter the health of the cell and its DNA.

"A new era has arrived where the future of anti-aging is focused on impacting living cells with nutrients and stimulating actives."

Skincare will become even more holistic. Even with topical anti-aging actives as the mainstay, nutritionists and lifestyle experts will continually achieve greater strides forward as information about the connection between skin and diet pours in at the speed of light. We will all become savvier about the types of diets and supplements that will enhance our skin, our health, and our well-being. We are on the cusp of discovering how healthy lifestyle upgrades can alter DNA for the better, and even increase longevity. What was once thought to be a foregone conclusion and fixed in stone—your fate and your DNA—is now within our reach through modern science.

As a parting thought, your skin's future is up to you. Keeping the forward-thinking spirit will go a long way—helping you keep yourself looking younger. Please refer to the pages in this book that describe the hierarchy of today's topicals, and start making good choices. And, most of all, whatever products you may happen to choose, please start using my THE SYSTEM: SMOOTH • STRENGTHEN • STIMULATE. You will see a tremendous change in your skin's appearance—guaranteed. And, most of all, remember that no matter what your age, because of modern science and forward thinkers, your best days are still ahead!

Nature, spirit, science— a powerful skin-saving three some!!

Chapter 9

THE BIRTH OF
BEAUTYPROOF®

09

THE BIRTH OF BEAUTYPROOF®

Skincare has rapidly evolved into much better treatments with much better results. A new era has arrived, and that's what this book is all about. The problem for the average person is that they haven't been privy to the latest advancements science has to offer. The complex biological process of aging is just that—complex. But the aim of this book is to make the complex logical and understandable for everyone. It is about ushering in a new era where women armed with knowledge can at last take control over their skin's destiny. They no longer have to accept the worn-out concept that just like taxes and death, wrinkles and old-looking skin are an inevitable fact of life. They just aren't.

As you may have read earlier, the light bulb moment igniting my endeavor to write this book emerged after I had completed my esthetician training and realized that most of the anti-aging skincare strategies—at least at that school—were still stuck in the Dark Ages. With my 20-plus years in the medical and pharmaceutical field, breaking down diseases and medicines to educate doctors and patients, I thought that at the very least I could provide information to help my co-estheticians. I wanted them to have access to the latest discoveries about the biology of aging and the hows and whys of today's modern active ingredients. One thing led to another, and instead of writing a book for only co-workers and other professionals in the skincare industry, I

decided to include the entire public. I wanted vital skin anti-aging information available to all, and especially to older women like myself.

It wasn't until I was almost finished with this book that I decided to found a new-era skincare company, BeautyProof®. The name? Beauty because I wanted all women to feel beautiful and empowered with the knowledge that aging skin can be controlled. And most of all, I wanted to deliver proof. I wanted to include powerful actives that stand on a firm ground of science before I included them in my formulations.

It wasn't easy finding the right chemist to work with. I found that many chemists are still stuck in the old days and resistant to incorporating ingredients they are unfamiliar with. Either they weren't knowledgeable about the newer active ingredients science has to offer, they didn't want to include effective amounts due to cost issues, or they were overly concerned about unusual colors some effective actives bring with them, such as red algae. Inertia had set in, and my quest was a long one.

But forward-thinking chemists were found! BeautyProof® was born, and I'm proud to say that it is a skincare company with one clear focus: anti-aging. All the products are built around impacting and reversing the biological processes that lead to aging skin.

What makes BeautyProof® different? I built my company on three simple, but powerful truths.

Truth #1:

BeautyProof® is not a one-hit wonder. The entire product line of many skincare companies is based around just one novel ingredient, often a patent to make their one-hit wonder sound like a miracle. Aging skin needs to be conquered on several levels. This requires an army of effective, proven active compounds, not just a few—or worse, one alone.

Truth #2:

BeautyProof® is all about anti-aging. No matter what your skin type, we will never pass on the anti-aging actives and focus entirely on your skin type. Everyone needs anti-aging treatments no matter what skin type they happen to have.

Truth #3:

BeautyProof® promises to stay on the forefront of anti-aging research. We seek out and deliver to you the most effective, forward-thinking ingredients the world has to offer. That's our promise to you.

BeautyProof® is also something much bigger—an inspiring way to look at the world. It is the realization that every day brings with it a new opportunity to be better than the last. Women today are more empowered than ever to make intelligent lifestyle, health, and, yes, even skincare decisions. Spirit combined with action can be a powerful combination. The BeautyProof® site is dedicated to bringing you new opportunities by presenting the latest scientific research and interviews from the most forward-thinking anti-aging experts on this planet.

Lesley Goodson
Author

Chapter 10

YOUR SURVIVAL KIT

THE SKIN PEARLS GLOSSARY

10

SMOOTHERS

CHEMICAL SMOOTHERS

• Alpha hydroxy acids

Glycolic acid is the most popular AHA.

Derived from sugarcane

10% strength is well documented to spur on collagen synthesis.

• Salicylic acids

Unique acid because it penetrates pores (lipid soluble).

Excellent for acne sufferers

• Fruit acids

Pumpkin, papaya, and pineapple

These fruit acids are especially mild and suited for sensitive skin.

PHYSICAL SMOOTHERS

• Synthetic (silicone) beads.

Although they are highly effective skin smoothers, they are harmful to the environment.

They pollute bodies of water and are ingested by marine life. Expect to see these banned in the future as there are ample natural skin smoothers that protect the environment. The following are the NATURAL ALTERNATIVES:

• Beads derived from lactic acid

• Natural ground bees wax

• Natural ground Carnauba wax

• Jojoba scrubbeads

• Zea mays

SMOOTHERS

BENEFITS OF NATURAL PHYSICAL SKIN SMOOTHERS

1. Provides a soft smooth feel

2. Visually improves skin texture and tone

3. Reduces the appearance of wrinkles and discourages new ones from forming

4. Long-term use has been shown to increase skin firmness.

5. Enhances penetration of skincare products

6. Increases cell turnover

7. Dismantles corneocyte plugs that cap and help wedge-in wrinkles

8. Promotes collagen, elastin, and hyaluronic acid due to signal mechanisms that induce the release of cytokines

ANTIOXIDANTS

ALGAE

• Marine algae has been used in skincare for thousands of years. With more than 28,000 different species, they are divided by color such as brown, red, green, and blue. Originally used for its inherent healing properties, scientists are just beginning to discover its many skin-saving benefits.

• Studies have demonstrated that some species of marine algae inhibit the surges in MMPs—metallo-proteinases—which are the enzymes that destroy healthy collagen matrixes and quickly cause wrinkle formation.

• It is also a top-selling skin brightener in Asia because of its skin lightening effects due to its inhibition of tyrosinase, an enzyme responsible for melanin formation.

ALPHA LIPOIC ACID

• A multi-tasking antioxidant

• Because it is both fat and water soluble, it is easily absorbed and works equally well on all parts of the cell.

• Apart from its antioxidant protection in all cellular parts, scientists are just beginning to discover its skin-lightening abilities. They have discovered it uses a different pathway to inhibit melanin synthesis and is, therefore, a good adjunct ingredient for skin lighteners.

ALNUS FIRMIFOLIA FRUIT EXTRACT

• The extract of the Japanese alder tree

• Touted to scavenge free radicals, inhibit MMPs, and stimulate DNA-repair enzymes

APPLE FRUIT EXTRACT

• A free-radical scavenger and source of malic acid, which is a gentle hydroxyl acid that aids in exfoliation.

• Use strictly for its gentle exfoliation benefits. As the Avicenna *Journal of Phytomedicine* concludes, it has weak to moderate to antioxidant ability at best.

ASPALATHUS LINEARIS LEAF EXTRACT

• Extract from the South African red bush rooibos

• Full of vitamins and minerals

AVOCADO OIL

• Persea gratissima—rich in vitamins A, D, E, potassium, and chlorine

• Penetrates extremely well due to the presence of palmitoleic acid

• Excellent ingredient for a dry-skin formulation

ASTAXANTHIN

• A red pigment found in shrimp and salmon

• Many times more effective than vitamin E, and also has proven photo-protective properties

• Two human studies looked at skin improvement when topical application was combined with oral supplementation of 6mg per day. All layers of skin—corneocyte, epidermis, and dermis—showed significant improvement. Crow's feet, wrinkles, dark spots, and elasticity, as well as trans-epidermal water loss, were improved by week eight.

VITAMIN B

• Enhances moisture and improves the barrier function and health of skin

• Guards against sallowness

VITAMIN B-3 NIACINAMIDE

• A water-soluble vitamin that effectively penetrates the stratum corneum and is extremely well tolerated

• It has been shown to prevent photo damage.

• It reduces trans-epidermal water loss indicating that it improves the barrier function. Because of this benefit, skin is more resistant to damaging detergents and sulfates.

• It reduces the appearance of dark spots in both Caucasian and Asian skin.

• It effectively inhibits yellowing or sallowness. Although the mechanism is not completely understood, it suppresses the age- and diet-related development of glycated collagen fibers that are responsible for much of yellowing skin.

• Small, but significant wrinkle reduction due to a small increase in collagen levels

• Look for a concentration of 5%.

VITAMIN B PANTHENOL

• Similar to niacinamide in that it is water soluble, it has been shown to increase lipid synthesis with the end result being an improved barrier function. You will experience improved hydration as well as improvement in roughness, scaling, and better tone to the epidermis.

• It minimally increases the number of collagen-producing cells, fibroblasts, and speeds wound healing.

• An effective anti-inflammatory

• Its hydration effects have led to its use in haircare products, promoting softness and elasticity.

VITAMIN C—THE GOLD STANDARD ANTIOXIDANT

Key Benefits

• Increases collagen synthesis—best results seen in L-ascorbic acid and MAP

• Photo protection. When applied before sun exposure, a 10% dose was shown to decrease UVB erythema by 54%.

• Lightens hyperpigmentation

• Anti-inflammatory

L-ASCORBIC ACID

• Vitamin C in the form of L-ascorbic acid must be applied before sun exposure to be protective.

• Most, but not all, formulations tend to be unstable in the presence of oxygen. Check for expiration dates. If purchasing a vitamin C serum, be sure to buy in small quantities. This will help ensure freshness. It should appear clear or white, never yellowed.

• Beware of manufacturers that add coloring to their vitamin C products. This makes it difficult for you, the consumer, to detect destabilization and diminishment of effectiveness.

• Look for strengths of 15% to 20%—lower strengths are not effective. If a 15% solution with a slightly acidic pH is applied daily, the level of vitamin C in the skin increases 20-fold and the skin tissue remains saturated for several days even if you stop using it. This is a benefit unique to this form of vitamin C. It also has been shown to inhibit the MMP enzymes responsible for collagen breakdown.

• May cause exfoliating effects for some users as most preparations need to be highly acidic to ensure proper penetration. Water soluble.

• If you cannot tolerate L-ascorbic acid, look for one of its derivatives such as those below.

ASCORBYL PALMITATE

• Because it is fat soluble, it is much better tolerated and more stable than L-ascorbic acid. In fact, it has a shelf life of two years.

• Has as strong an antioxidant effect as vitamin E, and is a highly effective anti-inflammatory.

• Although it has better tolerability, don't expect to see the same robust collagen synthesis as L-ascorbic acid, even at high concentrations.

MAGNESIUM ASCORBYL PHOSPHATE (MAP)

• Similar to ascorbyl palmitate MAP is a fat-soluble antioxidant. The benefit of being fat soluble is that it is non-irritating and more stable than vitamin C.

• It also appears to have similar collagen-producing benefits to L-ascorbic acid and is effective at much lower doses.

• M.A.P. is an excellent choice for people with sensitive skin.

COQ10

• When we age, the CoQ10 levels in skin are depleted. Because CoQ10 is a powerful antioxidant, our skin becomes prone to free-radical damage as our levels of it diminish.

• Some scientists theorize that energy loss, or in other words, impairment of mitochondrial function, is responsible for much of the aging process. Topical application has been shown to protect mitochondrial function.

- Small, but still significant, improvement in the depth of wrinkles has been demonstrated in well-designed studies.

- Similar to some forms of vitamin C, CoQ10 can become inactivated by oxygen. Buy in small quantities, preferably in airless containers.

CURCUMIN

- A polyphenol antioxidant derived from turmeric root

- Chemists have reported its antioxidant effects to be more powerful than vitamin E.

- Although the yellow color is undesirable in skin-care products, a hydrogenated off-white form is often used. You may see more of this potent antioxidant in the future.

VITAMIN E

- A free-radical scavenger known for its ability to penetrate the stratum corneum. Fat soluble.

- It is often used as a natural preservative and penetration enhancer in skincare products.

- Recall that it is a network antioxidant and, therefore, boosts efficacy of vitamin C as well as other antioxidants.

- It also provides some UV protection.

- Look for concentrations of at least 0.5%.

- If you take vitamin E orally, it is excreted in the sebaceous glands and uniquely provides protection from the inside out. You need to take consistently for a two-week period to reap the benefits.

EVENING PRIMROSE OIL

- Oenothera biennis—rich in linolenic acids. Also known as vitamin F

- When taken orally—3 X 500mg BID—skin moisture, TEWL, elasticity, firmness, fatigue resistance, and roughness significantly improved.

- Expect to start seeing results in 12 weeks.

GENISTEIN

- An active soy-free radical scavenger with several anti-aging properties.

- It inhibits destructive enzymes, fights glycated end products, and has been shown to stimulate collagen as well as partially repair the dermal-epidermal junction.

- An excellent skin strengthener for postmenopausal women as it binds weakly to estrogen receptors on skin cells.

- Women who opt out of hormone replacement therapy may well benefit from this ingredient.

GLUTATHIONE

- Probably the most important antioxidant in the body. Its diminishment has been linked to numerous diseases. Fat soluble.

- As a network antioxidant, it expands and extends the powerful benefits of most other antioxidants.

- Evidence points to a link between decreased glutathione levels and some signs of skin aging such as age spots.

- Consequently, it is now being used topically for its skin-lightening effects. Expect to be seeing much more about this powerful antioxidant in the near future.

- Unfortunately, it is extremely non-absorbable when taken in oral form. Many individuals opt for IV injections to remedy this disadvantage.

GRAPE SEED EXTRACT

• Vitis vinifera is viewed as a cancer preventative oral nutrient. It was in use as a topical treatment in earlier times.

• Its use as a wound healer dates back to European folk healers.

• It is now used for many beneficial properties such as anti-dandruff, anti-fungal, anti-microbial, and antioxidant.

• Also acts as a natural preservative.

IDEBENONE

• Originally discovered in an attempt to boost the therapeutic effects of CoQ10, it is closely related to CoQ10 in its structure. Fat soluble.

• No head-to-head studies comparing the two are available, but antioxidant levels of idebenone are considerably higher than CoQ10 as well as many other antioxidants.

VITAMIN K

• A vitamin that is naturally produced in the intestines and distributed throughout the body to aid in blood clotting.

• Look for at least a 5% dose to promote the evacuation of pooled blood from the skin. It will reduce redness as well as bruising.

LYCOPENE

• Many of us are aware of the many health benefits of lycopene found primarily in tomatoes. One of its antioxidant effects is protection from UV rays, or in more technical terms, protection against UVR induced erythema.

• Please be advised that cooked or canned tomatoes are a better source of lycopene.

• However, dietary intake may not be enough to maximize skin benefits. When ingested, only small amounts make its way to the skin. Luckily, lycopene is well absorbed if applied topically. Expect to experience benefits in skin roughness.

NIACINAMIDE

• See vitamin B.

PINE BARK

• Pycnogenol is a water-soluble antioxidant derived from the extract of French marine bark.

• Pycnogenol is well absorbed in skin.

• Because it contains several phenolic constituents, it is a potent free-radical scavenger with several other benefits. It has been shown to accelerate wound healing and lower scar formation. It protects not only from UV-induced edema, but UV-induced tumor formation as well. Of particular note is its ability to shut down the enzymes that accelerate collagen degradation.

RESVERATROL

• A chemical cousin to curcumin, it is a polyphenol found in the skin of grapes.

• A highly potent antioxidant as well as an anti-inflammatory agent. In fact, several studies have found it to be one of the most potent antioxidants to date. Although even the best-designed studies may conflict with others, several studies suggest that resveratrol possesses a 17-fold greater antioxidant potency than idebenone. Once hailed as untouchably potent, idebenone is a powerful pharmaceutical antioxidant.

- Resveratrol protects against both UVA and UVB damage.

- A go-to antioxidant if you cannot tolerate vitamin C with vitamin E.

SOY

- Soybeans are a rich source of antioxidant flavonoids. Look for such names as genistein and daidzein. They are also classified as plant estrogens as the soy derivatives have chemical structures similar to human estrogen, and weakly bind to estrogen skin receptors.

- Estrogens increase skin thickness by promoting collagen synthesis. They also have been reported to rebuild the proteins supporting the dermal-epidermal junction and help fight against creppy, fragile skin.

- Beyond its antioxidant ability, soy appears to be a safe and effective treatment for postmenopausal women whose estrogen levels have dropped dramatically. Due to the drop in levels, their skin quickly thinned and significantly dried. Serious wrinkles develop quickly. Soy proteins called phytoestrogens interact with skin cells similar to a woman's own estrogen.

- It is also effective for a hyperpigmentation disorders. Soy compounds prevent melanin pigments from adhering to skin cells which is why genistein is used in skin-lightening creams.

- Keep in mind that genistein is most effective when hyperpigmentation is caused by UV rays, and not caused by hormones. It does not work for melasma because melasma is fueled by the hormone estrogen and genistein is almost identical to an estrogen.

SOD

- Superoxide dismutase (SOD)—similar to CoQ10—protects your skin cells' energy factories called mitochondria. As mentioned in the CoQ10 description, some researchers postulate that skin aging is accelerated due to loss of energy output when the mitochondria is impaired by free radicals.

- Studies have indicated that SOD's mitochondrial protection does have long-term anti-aging qualities such as maintaining the lifespan of healthy fibroblasts, the cells that create your youthful supportive collagen matrix. Fat soluble.

TAURINE

- A powerful antioxidant as well as glycation inhibitor

- Glycation occurs when sugars attach to collagen fibers which ultimately reduces the collagen regenerative properties. This in turn promotes wrinkles, sagging, and a yellowed-skin appearance.

- This potent glycation inhibitor is now being studied for its ability to delay diabetic skin complications.

ZEAXANTHIN

- A fat-soluble carotenoid similar to lutein in its ability to counteract the aging effects of sun exposure

- Most studies look at DNA protection against UV radiation using oral supplements. They often recommend that the highest degree of antioxidant protection is achieved using both oral and topical administration.

ZINC

ZINC GLUCONATE

• Assists in regulating sebaceous glands

ZINC OXIDE

• A sun protectant against aging UVA rays. It also has anti-irritant and antioxidant properties.

• Has been shown to provide superior protection against UVA when compared to titanium dioxide.

ZINC-COPPER MALONATE

• Has shown robust regeneration of elastic tissue in patients with sun-damaged skin. Look for this unique anti-wrinkle agent to appear in future skincare preparations.

ANTI-INFLAMMATORIES

ALLANTOIN

Used for its anti-inflammatory properties as well as its moisturizing effect. It increases the smoothness of skin and aids in the wound-healing process.

ALOE VERA

Probably one of the most widely used botanical compounds to date. Besides reduced inflammation, aloe vera increases blood flow, decreases bacterial colonization, and enhances wound healing. Rich in amino acids, glycosides, mucopolyaccharides, and minerals to name just a few. The plant has a whopping 75 different nutrients and clinical data supports its anti-aging benefits, but a definitive dose threshold has not yet been established.

BOERHAVIA DIFFUSA ROOT EXTRACT

An Indian plant that possesses anti-inflammatory properties to sooth irritated and sensitive skin. Suppresses inflammation upstream by limiting the chemical mediators that start the inflammatory cascade.

CAMELLIA SINENSIS LEAF EXTRACT

Both a powerful antioxidant as well as anti-inflammatory agent. Helps to control the activation of collagen damaging enzymes (MMPs).

CENTAUREA CYANUS FLOWER EXTRACT

Similar to chamomile, this extract is known to soothe and calm skin.

CHAMOMILE FLOWER EXTRACT

Highly soothing, anti-inflammatory extract with skin-healing properties. Blue chamomile, or azulene, is an active ingredient in chamomile that is produced during the distillation process.

CUCUMBER

Animal studies suggest that cucumbers reduce inflammation by inhibiting enzymes that spark the inflammatory cascade. Also contains the antioxidants vitamin C and beta-carotene.

ECHINACEA EXTRACT

Native to North America and used as traditional herbal remedies to treat boils, abscesses, burns, and skin ulcers.

GERANIUM OIL

Roots from the plant are used for its anti-inflammatory and soothing properties. Effective for skin irritations and dermatitis.

GINKO BILOBA

A potent anti-inflammatory. Many of its beneficial anti-aging effects are thanks to its high levels of quercetin, a common and powerful antioxidant. It has been discovered to treat inflammatory conditions such as acne, eczema, and other types of facial redness and irritation. Studies have indicated it improves microcirculation as it protects capillaries against fragility. It also increases blood flow, boosting oxygen levels. This effect is attributable to its properties as a vasodilator.

GOTU KOLA

In India, gotu kola, also known as centella asiatica, is considered to be a spiritual herb. Growing in some areas of the Himalayas, gotu kola is used by some yogis to improve meditation. It reduces scarring when applied during the inflammatory period of the wound. Also used to treat burns, gotu kola is now considered to be an effective and natural alternative treatment for hyperpigmentation.

GREEN TEA

A superhero anti-inflammatory as well as antioxidant. The polyphenol antioxidants in green tea have also been shown to help prevent certain skin cancers and protect skin against sunburn. They are also being studied for possible cancer-fighting potential, but thus far results are inconclusive. However, there have been studies that show the antioxidants in green tea protect the DNA in skin cells.

LAVENDER

Lavender has antiseptic and anti-inflammatory properties. It helps skin heal more quickly and with less scarring. The soothing and anti-inflammatory action of lavender oil will also have a balancing action on the skin and can be used for dermatitis, eczema, and psoriasis.

LICORICE ROOT

Licorice extract, also known as dipotassium glycyrrhizate, has been used for its health benefits as far back as ancient China. It contains beneficial plant sterols which promote skin elasticity and fight inflammation. Licorice extract is so powerful that it can soothe problems caused by irritating skincare products.

MILK THISTLE

Silymarin belongs to a family of plants that include daisies, thistles, and artichokes. It has been used for centuries as a detoxifying herb. Not a lot is known about milk thistle as a topical skin anti-ager, but studies have shown it to protect against UV damage. In addition to these effects, milk thistle also soothes and moistens the skin, while calming any inflammation. Patients with skin problems like eczema and acne, rosacea, cracking skin, and dry skin may notice a difference when using milk thistle formulations. In fact, in one double-blind study on patients suffering from State I-III rosacea, those treated with a topical cream containing silymarin experienced significant improvement in redness, papules, itching, hydration, and skin color.

MORUS ALBA ROOT EXTRACT

A native plant of Japan. It is a treatment for hyperpigmentation as well as an anti-inflammatory agent.

MUGWORT EXTRACT

Also known as artemisia vulgaris extract, is an effective anti-inflammatory as well as anti-irritant. This active is known to reduce redness.

MUSHROOM EXTRACT

Also known as cordyceps sinensis extract, it is known to reduce both short- and long-term inflammation.

OAT BETA GLUCAN

Capable of penetrating deep into the skin and delivering anti-inflammatory and other anti-aging benefits. It works as an anti-irritant and speeds wound healing. Oat beta glucan is found in natural sources such as cereals and yeast. A 2005 study showed that it penetrated to the dermis which is the layer where wrinkles form. Split face trials do confirm its anti-aging effects on wrinkles, roughness, and firmness.

POMEGRANATE

A powerful antioxidant and anti-inflammatory. At least 40% levels help protect against sun damage and cancerous changes due to UV exposure.

PORTULACA OLERACEA EXTRACT

An enriched extract of vitamins, fatty acids, flavonoids, and anti-inflammatory agents that help control and reduce redness. In the *Australian Journal of Medical Herbalism*, a review of portulaca stated that it accelerates the healing process of wounds.

PRICKLY PEAR

Also known as cactus pear, prickly pear is native to the American Southwest desert. After the Europeans settled, it was imported to Europe as a salve designed to soothe cutaneous wounds and burns. The fleshy pad of the pear was rubbed over skin surfaces to act as a moisturizer, imparting a soothing effect. When the substance evaporated, the protective coating acted as a partial sunscreen.

SEA KELP

Sea Kelp is often fermented to increase the bioavailability of its many chemical compounds. Amazingly versatile, it can be found in a variety of skincare products for its moisturizing and anti-inflammatory properties.

SILANEDIOL SALICYLATE

Soothes skin and acts as an antioxidant as well as an anti-inflammatory. Helps prevent the release of destructive inflammatory mediators during the inflammatory cascade.

ST JOHN'S WORT

Also known as hypericum perforatum extract, its history dates back to ancient Greece. Used as an antidepressant when taken orally, for skincare it has been shown to be antibacterial as well as anti-inflammatory. Also aids in wound healing.

YUCCA SCHIDIGERA EXTRACT

Derived from the cactus plant known as yucca. Used to treat burns and mild abrasions. Yucca root has phytosterols. Studies indicate yucca extract has anti-inflammatory and antioxidant qualities

COLLAGEN KEEPERS

GLYCATION INHIBITORS

Glycation, or consuming a diet high in sugars and refined carbohydrates, not only damages your existing collagen, but it dramatically impairs future collagen production and elastin metabolism. It keeps the collagen molecules from forming a network-like structure.

The effects of a sugary diet manifest themselves by the age of 35. Skin becomes more yellowed in appearance, with fine lines and loss of tone. Ever notice the yellow complexions of chain smokers? It is believed that cigarette smoke can increase the speed of the glycation process. Yet another reason to stay away from second-hand smoke.

The following actives are able to inhibit the sugars from binding to your collagen proteins. You will be hearing more about these collagen keepers in the future.

- **Blueberries**
- **Carnosine**
- **Pomegranate**
- **Vitamin C**
- **Green tea**

MMP INHIBITORS

MMP inhibitors (MMPIs) are actives that prevent or inhibit the effects of metalloproteinase enzymes—MMPs—which are responsible for aging and destroying your collagen elastin network. Remember that this network is responsible for firmness, strength, suppleness, and smoothness of your skin! In short, this matrix—or safety net—is one of the most-important commodities you've got and you need to protect your assets! As our ability to respond to stimulators such as peptides and retinoids declines as we age, these agents become an increasingly important component of our skincare regimen.

MMPs are most often activated after sun exposure or any other event that will increase the free-radical levels and inflammation in your skin, such as chlorinated water and exposure to second-hand cigarette smoke. That is why some anti-inflammatory actives such as green tea have been shown to effectively spare skin from the devastating effects of these enzymes.

Unfortunately for drug companies, the development of effective MMP inhibitors has met with limited success. Ensuring your skincare contains a blend of antioxidants and anti-inflammatory actives, coupled with strict sun avoidance, will be the best way to keep your safety net strong, smooth, and firm.

Glycation and MMP inhibitors go a long way to protect your skin's natural collagen matrix. Our collagen safety nets are what keep our skin youthful, firm, and wrinkle free. As we get older, our skin becomes less able to produce this valuable commodity, making protecting what we already have extremely important.

STIMULATORS

ALPHA HYDROXY ACIDS

The differences you should know about.

All acids act in similar ways. They all help dissolve the glue or cement that holds your outer, dead and hardened skin cells together. As you know, I am not a proponent of using a mild acid peel as your daily smoother because they can be tricky to use and the results are mixed.

However, there is a lot of good news surrounding acids, specifically alpha hydroxy and beta hydroxy acids. Both can be very effective tools in the war against wrinkles. You just need to know which one to choose if you are fighting off wrinkles, enlarged pores, or even age spots.

GLYCOLIC ACID

Let's start with one of my favorite alpha hydroxy acids (AHAs), glycolic acid. Made from sugar cane, glycolic acid is the only AHA able to penetrate through cell walls by virtue of its small molecular size. At a dose of 10% or higher, it can trigger new formation of collagen and turn on the synthesis of an important moisture binding cell, glycosaminoglycan. The result is a cellular plumping effect, as well as the reduction of fine wrinkles. Remember that you need 10% or higher concentration of this ingredient if you are looking for increased smoothness of skin texture, wrinkle reduction, enhanced penetration of added topicals such as skin lighteners, and general revitalizing of your skin.

LACTIC ACID

If you find glycolic acid too irritating, lactic acid is a great alternative. Lactic acid, derived from milk, is a natural humectant. This means that it can pull moisture from the air into the skin. Lactic acid is increasingly showing up in body moisturizers. Body skin can be more difficult to treat because of an overabundance of dead cell buildup, resulting in excessively dry scaly skin. Lactic acid helps break apart this wall of dead cells and then attract moisture to the site.

SALICYLIC ACID

Salicylic acid may well be a superior exfoliator when compared to the two commonly used acids listed above. This is because salicylic acid is fat soluble and able to deeply penetrate skin pores, as well as exfoliate surface skin. Because of this fact, just a small percentage of salicylic acid is required for anyone with acne or who wants to shrink pore size. Much higher dosages have been used as professional peels for these results:

• Diminish the appearance of fine lines by stimulating collagen production

• Visibly reduce pore size

• Even skin tone and help minimize discolorations

• Effectively treat acne and environmental sun damage

• Deliver cumulative benefits and optimal results with weekly/monthly treatments

GROWTH FACTORS

Epidermal growth factor (EGF), also known simply as growth factors, was a major anti-aging discovery dating all the way back to 1986. The two scientists who discovered EGF were awarded a Nobel Prize in medicine for their work, which opened the door for understanding how cells communicate with one another. This forever changed the landscape of anti-aging skincare, and since then, companies have endeavored to develop even better growth factor formulations.

Although most of the research into growth factors was in the arena of wound repair, research has shown that, when growth factors are combined with other skin stimulators, the results can be dramatic.

Like hormones, growth factors are chemical messengers. How do they communicate? Similar to hormones, growth factors trigger cells into action by fitting into tiny growth factor receptors on the outside or membrane of the cell. Among its many skin-regenerating properties is the revving up of your fibroblasts—the cells that produce collagen. When fibroblasts are stimulated, they synthesize more collagen and that's what you want to keep your skin firm and wrinkle free.

Keep in mind that when we age, our natural levels of growth factors decline significantly. In addition, our natural production of EGF significantly slows when UV light is present, hindering the body's ability to repair itself. Just another reason to avoid sun exposure!

Since the initial discovery of EGF, a multitude of growth factors have been added to highly sophisticated skincare formulations. One company touted as having the most-advanced growth factor formulations is Skin Medica. Expensive, yes, but the results are impressive.

STIMULATORS

HORMONES

In our modern age, many people do not recognize the significant increase in life expectancy we have experienced over the decades. At the time our nation was born and we elected our first president, George Washington, the average life expectancy was only 35 years. Today, in the United States, individuals live an average of 78 years. We have, without a doubt, benefited from all the scientific research into curing and treating a variety of age-related diseases. Yet, our quality of life has declined significantly. Loss of energy and stamina, muscle tone, and bone mass, to name a few. The culprit? Hormones, or rather the decreasing levels we all experience as the years pile up.

What does this have to do with our skin? Just as you read in the Growth Factor Skin Pearls, hormones are chemical messengers that trigger or stimulate other cells to do things. In the case of skin, your hormones attach to tiny receptors on your skin cells and keep them young. As you've read in the Hormone chapter, when we experience menopause, women take a tremendous hit to our skin. The loss of collagen is enormous.

Studies show that hormone replacement can restore quality of life. With life expectancy higher than ever, we need to reconsider how we are going to experience our golden years. HRT, or hormone replacement therapy through the use of bio-identical hormones, is now becoming more the norm rather than the exception. Studies also confirm a rejuvenating effect on skin, although only a minor one if your skin is excessively sun damaged. Retin-A and retinaldehyde are the proven winners if that is your primary concern.

Please refer to my interview with one of the nation's top experts in the field of anti-aging medicine and bio-identical hormones, Dr. Selma Rashid. It could be a missing link to getting quality back into your life—better mood, vitality, bone mass, and energy. And, of course, its ability to stimulate skin cells into acting youthfully. Just one of its many benefits!

PEPTIDES

Peptides are short chains of amino acids. When you see the word peptide placed on a container, do not assume they all produce the same results or work in the same manner. Here are the similarities and the differences.

SIGNAL PEPTIDES

These peptides directly stimulate fibroblasts to generate more collagen. Because they mimic fragments of damaged, broken collagen or short amino acid chains, your fibroblasts—the collagen manufacturers—think that skin is damaged and needs to repair itself. The end result is that fibroblasts become activated and your skin produces more of what it needs to stay young looking.

Collagen is created by fibroblasts, which are specialized skin cells located in the dermis. Fibroblasts also produce other skin-structural proteins such as elastin—a protein which gives the skin its ability to snap back—and glucosaminoglycans (GAGs). GAGs make up the ground substance that keeps the dermis hydrated. Signal peptides also inhibit your skin's enzymes that break down collagen and elastin.

PEARLS

One of the most-effective signal peptides is an ingredient trademarked Matrixyl 3000. It is a combination of a GHK peptide and a fatty-acid peptide called palmitic acid. The fatty acid portion improves penetration of the product. The GHK peptide is a fragment of type I collagen and a proven stimulator of fibroblasts. Other effective peptides include Syn-Coll, Trylagen, Syn-Hycan, and Pepha Tight.

CARRIER PEPTIDES

Another function of peptides is to stabilize and deliver metals such as copper, an important trace element necessary for the wound-healing process. It also activates skin remodeling, has antioxidant properties, and can produce beneficial outcomes on the structural collagen matrix.

PEARLS

Look for a copper peptide with GHK-Cu lettering in the name. That indicates that not only does it act as a signal peptide (GHK), but it also delivers copper (Cu).

NEUROTRANSMITTER PEPTIDES

Neurotransmitter peptides block the release of neurotransmitters—chemical messengers—from neurons to muscles. Because these neurotransmitters are necessary for muscle contraction, neurotransmitter-modulating peptides such as Argireline work to relax the muscles near the top of the skin. There is currently a lot of buzz around this type of peptide. Any time you read that a product relaxes wrinkles, chances are that it contains a neurotransmitter peptide.

PEARLS

This is an ingredient that has short-term, temporary, and modest anti-wrinkle effect at best. The key word is temporary. You want your skin to grow younger, not just relax a bit for an 8-hour period. It doesn't hurt to have it included in a formulation. Just have a closer look at the ingredient list to ensure other potent actives such as signal peptides like Matrixyl are listed as well. If the marketing claim is "Botox in a bottle," it probably indicates that only this type of peptide is included and is not a good investment if you seriously want to repair your skin. Examples of peptides in this category include Argireline, Leuphasyl, Snap-8, and Syn-Ake.

If you want to smooth and relax expression wrinkles, Botox is highly effective and worth the expense. It is a better choice if you have severe crow's feet or forehead furrows. Because it relaxes the deeper facial muscles, where peptides can't reach, the results are much more pronounced. It also works 24/7, and over a long period of time it can give you an added edge in erasing wrinkles. Over time, you will need less Botox—and eventually no Botox at all—as your skin rejuvenates and repairs itself by using your THE SYSTEM treatment plan.

RETINOIDS

Retin-A, or the generic form tretinoin, is the most-effective anti-aging active on the market today because it remodels skin on a cellular level. It not only reverses sun damage, but it also has been proven to reverse intrinsic aging, which was once believed to be irreversible. It does so through the following mechanisms:

It reduces MMPs, the enzymes that break down the collagen network, resulting in wrinkles and sagging as a consequence of the down regulation of transcription factors.

It stimulates fibroblasts to repair photo-aged skin by activating the synthesis of collagens, fibrillins, and glycosaminoglycans (GAGs), or moisture-binding skin cells.

It removes structured collagen around the base of the wrinkle while new collagen and other molecules are deposited correctly as the wrinkle diminishes.

PEARLS

You may have been told that your store-bought retinol is as effective as prescription retinol without the irritation, but actual results with store-bought retinols are modest at best.

In order for your store-bought retinol to be as effective a wrinkle reducer as prescription Retin-A, your skin needs to convert the retinol into Retin-A, or tretinoin. This conversion process is complex, and the retinol you put on your skin has a long route to the finish line where it is able to lock itself inside the cell receptors and do its magic. Unfortunately, the conversion rate is low, and it varies among individuals. Here's what it looks like:

Retinyl palimate. Although more tolerable than the other retinoids, it has weak efficacy because it takes three separate conversion steps to become effective. It is considered to be 20 times less effective than Retin-A. Expect minimal benefits.

Retinol. More effective that retinyl palimate, but more effective only because it takes two conversion steps and not three to become effective. Moderate anti-aging effects can be seen if large dosages are used.

Retinaldahyde. Only one conversion step away from Retin–A. Comparative studies against Retin-A show similar anti-aging effects, but with much fewer side effects. Perhaps due to its higher cost, few skincare companies incorporate it into their product lines.

Retin-A. Because your skin doesn't need to convert it, Retin-A has direct access to the skin cell receptors. You get the full benefit of the anti-aging active, but this doesn't come without a price. During the initial weeks and even months, expect side effects of skin flaking and irritation.

Strictly follow your doctor's advice regarding usage. You may need at least six weeks to see substantial benefits. Be patient. Start at a low dosage, mixing a small amount in your moisturizer and increasing the amount slowly. Try using once a week at first, and after a period of time, increase to three times a week. Do not use if you are pregnant, have rosacea, or are using potential irritants such as glycolic acid. Expect to see dramatic improvement in about 24 weeks. It's not a quick fix, but if you can overcome the side effects and be patient, the results speak for themselves. It is a heavy hitter in maintaining young skin for life.

Retinaldahyde is your next-best alternative, and it doesn't carry with it the side effects associated with Retin-A. Early studies show a profound impact on repairing aging skin.

BIBLIOGRAP

Bauza E et al., Collagen-like peptide exhibits a remarkable antiwrinkle effect on the skin when topically applied: in vivo study. Int J Tissue React. 2004;26(3-4):105-11.

Bennett MF et al., Skin immune systems and inflammation: protector of the skin or promoter of aging? J Investig Dermatol Symp Proc. 2008 Apr;13(1):15-9.

Brincat MP et al., Estrogens and the skin. Climacteric 2005 Jun:8(2):110-23

Chan, WH et al., Curcumin Inhibits UV Irradiation-Induced Oxidative

Stress and Apoptotic Biochemical Changes in Human Epidermoid Carcinoma A431 Cells. Journal of Cellular Biochemistry 90:327–338 (2003)

Chen Y et al., Brain-skin connection: stress, inflammation and skin aging. Inflamm Allergy Drug Targets. 2014;13(3):177-90.

Contet-Audonneau, JL et al., A histological study of human wrinkle structures: comparison between sun-exposed areas of the face, with or without wrinkles, and sun-protected areas. British Journal of Dermatology 1999; 140: 1038–1047

Cosgrove MC et al., Dietary nutrient intakes and skin-aging appearance among middle-aged American women. Am J Clin Nutr. 2007 Oct;86(4):1225-31.

Chung JH et al., Modulation of skin collagen metabolism in aged and photoaged human skin in vivo. J Invest Dermatol. 2001 Nov;117(5):1218-24.

Danby FW, Nutrition and aging skin: sugar and glycation, Clin Dermatol. 2010 Jul-Aug;28(4):409-11

Dong KK et al., UV-induced DNA damage initiates release of MMP-1 in human skin. Experimental Dermatology 2008 De:17(12):1037-44

Draelos Z, Botanical Antioxidants. Cosmetic Dermatology. 2003 16:46-48

Farage, M. et al., Textbook of Aging Skin. Jan 22, 2010.

Farris PK, Topical vitamin C: a useful agent for treating photoaging and other dermatologic conditions. Dermatol Surg. 2005 Jul;31(7 Pt 2):814-7

Fisher GJ et al., Collagen fragmentation promotes oxidative stress and elevates matrix metalloproteinases-1 in fibroblasts in aged human skin. Am J Pathol. 2009 January; 174(1): 101-114

Fisher et al., Looking older: Fibroblast Collapse and Therapeutic Implications. Arch Dermatol. 2008 May; 144(5): 666-672

Fisher G et al., 'Molecular Mechanisms of Photoaging in Human Skin In Vivo and Their Prevention by All-Trans Retinoic Acid. Photochemistry and Photobiology. 1999, 69(2): 154-1 57

Fisher et al., Pathophysiology of Premature Skin Aging Induced By Ultraviolet Light. N Engl J Med. 1997; 337:1419-1429 November 13, 1997

Fisher GJ et al., Mechanisms of photo aging and chronological skin aging. Arch Dermatol. 2002 Nov:138(11):1462-70

Giacomoni PU et al., Factors of skin ageing share common mechanisms. Biogerontology. 2001;2(4):219-29.

Gilchrest BA et al., Skin Aging. Springer-Verlag. Berlin Heidelberg 2006

Greul AK et al., Photoprotection of UV-irradiated human skin: an antioxidative combination of vitamins E and C, carotenoids, selenium and proanthocyanidins. Skin Pharmacol Appl Skin Physiol. 2002 Sep-Oct:15(5):307-15

Y

Griffiths CE et al., Restoration of collagen formation in photo damaged human skin by tretinoin (retinoic acid). N Engl J Med. 1993 Aug 19:329(8):530-5

Hall G et al., Estrogen and skin: the effects of estrogen, menopause, and hormone replacement therapy on the skin. J Am Acad Dermatol. 2005 Oct:53(4):555-68

Han B et al., Transdermal delivery of amino acids and antioxidants enhance collagen synthesis: in vivo and in vitro studies. Connect Tissue Res. 2005;46(4-5):251-7.

Hashizume H, Skin aging and dry skin. J Dermatol. 2004 Aug;31(8):603-9

Hubbard BA et al., Reversal of skin aging with topical retinoids. Plast Reconstr Surg. 2014 Apr;133(4):481

Hughes MC et al., Sunscreen and prevention of skin aging: a randomized trial. Ann Intern Med. 2013 Jun 4;158(11):781-90

Ichihashi, M et al., Introduction Glycation Stress and Photo-Aging in Skin. Anti-Aging Medicine 8; 23-29: 2011

Katiyar SK et al., Green tea polyphenols: DNA photodamage and photoimmunology. J Photochem Photobiol B. 2001 Dec 31;65(2-3):109-14.

Katiyar SK et al., Polyphenolic antioxidant (-)-epi-gallocatechin-3-gallate from green tea reduces UVB-induced inflammatory responses and infiltration of leukocytes in human skin. Photochem Photobiol. 1999 Feb;69(2):148-53.

Kim SJ et al., The effect of glycolic acid on cultured human skin fibroblasts: cell proliferative effect and increased collagen synthesis. J Dermatol. 1998 Feb;25(2):85-9.

Kligman AM et al., Topical tretinoin for photoaged skin. J Am Acad Dermatol. 1986 Oct:15(4 Pt 2):836-59

Knuutinen A et al., Smoking affects collagen synthesis and extracellular matrix turnover in human skin. Br J Dermatol. 2002 Apr;146(4):588-94.

Lanuti,EL et al., Effects of Pollution on Skin Aging. Journal of Investigative Dermatology. (2010) 130, 2696. doi:10.1038/jid.2010.323

Lohwasser Christina et al., The Receptor for Advanced Glycation End Products Is Highly Expressed in the Skin and Upregulated by Advanced Glycation End Products and Tumor Necrosis Factor-Alpha. Journal of Investigative Dermatology. (2006) 126, 291–299. doi:10.1038/sj.jid.5700070; published online 22 December 2005

Marini A et al., Pycnogenol® effects on skin elasticity and hydration coincide with increased gene expressions of collagen type I and hyaluronic acid synthase in women. Skin Pharmacol Physiol. 2012;25(2):86-92

McCullough JL, Prevention and treatment of skin aging. Ann NY Acad Sci. 2006 May;1067:323-31.

Morita A et al., Molecular basis of tobacco smoke-induced premature skin aging. J Investig Dermatol Symp Proc. 2009 Aug;14(1):53-5.

Mukherjee S et al., Retinoids in the treatment of skin aging: an overview of clinical efficacy and safety. Clin Interv Aging. 2006 Dec; 1(4): 327–348.

Oba C et al., Collagen hydrolysate intake improves the loss of epidermal barrier function and skin elasticity induced by UVB irradiation in hairless mice. Photodermatol Photoimmunol Photomed. 2013 Aug;29(4):204-11

Pandel R et al., Skin Photoaging and the Role of Antioxidants in Its Prevention. ISRN Dermatology. Volume 2013 (2013), Article ID 930164, 11

Papakonstantinou E et al., Hyaluronic acid: A key molecule in skin aging. Dermatoendocrinol. 2012 Jul 1;4(3):253-8

Perricone NV, Topical vitamin C ester (ascorbyl palimate). Journal of Geriatric Dermatology. 5:162-170

Pietropaoli D, Advanced glycation end products: possible link between metabolic syndrome and periodontal diseases. Int J Immunopathol Pharmacol. 2012 Jan-Mar;25(1):9-17.

Pinnell SR, Cutaneous photodamage, oxidative stress and topical antioxidant protection. Journal of American Academy of Dermatology. 2003 48:1-19

Pinnell SR, Yang HS, Omar M, et al Topical L-ascorbic acid percutaneous absorption studies. Dermatologic Surgery. 2001 27:137-142

Proksch E et al., Oral supplementation of specific collagen peptides has beneficial effects on human skin physiology. Skin Pharmacol Physiol. 2014;27(1):47-55

Puizina-Ivi N et al., Modern approach to topical treatment of aging skin. Coll Antropol. 2010 Sep;34(3):1145-53.

Quan T et al., Matrix-degrading metalloproteinases in photoaging. Journal of Investigative Dermatological Symposim Proc. 2009 14(1): 20-24

Quan T et al., Solar ultraviolet irradiation reduces collagen in photoaged human skin by blocking transforming growth factor-beta type II receptor/Smad signaling. Am J Pathol. 2004 Sep;165(3):741-51.

Raine-Fenning NJ et al., Skin aging and menopause: implications for treatment. Am J Clin Dermatol. 2003:4(6):371-8

Rittié L et al., Induction of collagen by estradiol: difference between sun-protected and photodamaged human skin in vivo. Arch Dermatol. 2008 Sep;144(9):1129-40.

Saewan N et al., Natural products as photoprotection. J Cosmet Dermatol. 2015 Jan 12. doi: 10.1111/jocd.12123.

Saokar, P et al., Vitamin C in dermatology. Indian Dermatol Online J. 2013 Apr-Jun; 4(2): 143–146.

Sator PG et al., Skin Treatments and Dermatological Procedures to Promote Youthful Skin. Clin Interv Aging. 2006;1(1):51-6

Sauermann, K et al., Topically applied vitamin C increases the density of dermal papillae in aged human skin. Journal of Investigative Dermatology. (2010) 130, 2696.

Schagen SK, Discovering the link between nutrition and skin aging. Dermatoendocrinol. 2012 Jul 1;4(3):298-307

Schmidt JB et al., Treatment of skin aging with topical estrogens. Int J Dermatol. 1996 Sep;35(9):669-74.

Shah MG et al., Estrogen and skin. An overview. Am J Clin Dermatol. 2001;2(3):143-50.

Shuster, S et al., The influence of age and sex on skin thickness, skin collagen and density. British Journal of Dermatology. Jul 2006

Telang PS et al., Vitamin C in dermatology. Indian Dermatol Online J. 2013 Apr-Jun; 4(2): 143–146

Tournas JA, Fu-Hsiung L, Burch JA et al., Ubiqui-none, idebenone and kinetin provide ineffective photoprotection to skin when compared to topical antioxidant combination of vitamins C and E with ferulic acid. Journal of Investigative Dermatology. 2006 126:1185-7

Varani J, Decreased Collagen Production in Chrono-logically Aged Skin. Am J Pathol. 2006 Jun; 168(6): 1861–1868

Varani J, Inhibition of type I procollagen synthesis by damaged collagen in photoaged skin and by col-lagenase-degraded collagen in vitro. Am J Pathol. 2001 Mar;158(3):931-42.

Vayali PK et al., Green tea polyphenols prevent ul-traviolet light-induced oxidative damage and matrix metalloproteinases expression in mouse skin. J Invest Dermatol. 2004 Jun;122(6):1480-7.

Watson S et al., A Cosmetic 'Anti-ageing' Product Improves Photoaged Skin: A Double-blind, Random-ized Controlled Trial. The British Journal of Dermatol-ogy. 2009;161(2):419-426.

Wang B et al., Isolation and Characterization of Collagen and Antioxidant Collagen Peptides from Scales of Croceine Croaker (Pseudosciaena crocea). Mar Drugs. 2013 Nov; 11(11)

BIOGRAPHIE

LESLEY GOODSON

Lesley has spent a lifetime helping women recapture their youthful skin. Throughout her long career in medicine, she never gave up on her quest to uncover and share remarkable studies and research that answer what she calls -The Million Dollar Question - Is Aging Skin Inevitable? According to Lesley and many of her clients, the answer is no! Young skin for life should be the new normal, not the exception. "I love sharing what I consider to be precious — the honest science. It empowers women to feel happier and look younger and more beautiful. It's what I do."

Lesley earned her BA in French, MBA in marketing and enjoyed a decade's long career in the field of medicine. She is the recipient of many national awards for her expertise in medicine, research and marketing. She is also a black belt in shitoryu karate and a national medalist. She resides in Florida with her husband Pierre, a leader in the aerospace industry – not once- but twice- awarded by the governor for his remarkable job creation program. "Those are moments I will never forget. I am incredibly proud of how he has helped so many Floridian families."

BeautyProof.com

SHOGO OTA

In 2012, Shogo Ota, established Tireman Studio, a Seattle based graphic design and art company. An acclaimed artist in his own right, Starbucks has commissioned his work to appear in multiple projects –from a hand painted mural to a series of posters. His work has also been featured in The Stranger, ZIIBRA, Print magazine, The Seattle-Havana-Tehran Poster Show and various other publications. Shogo and his wife recently gave birth and to a beautiful baby boy.
Shogo can be contacted at:

TiremanStudio.com.

PETER ECONOMY

Peter Economy is a best-selling business author, ghostwriter, developmental editor, and publishing consultant with more than 80 books to his credit (and more than 2 million copies sold), including *Everything I Learned About Life I Learned in Dance Class; Story Mapping: Discover the Whole Story, Build the Right Product; Managing For Dummies; The Management Bible*; and many more. Peter is also the Leadership Guy on Inc.com and associate editor for Leader to Leader magazine. Learn more at:

PeterEconomy.com.